LIGHT
THE SKY

COMEDY IN THREE ACTS
BY MOSS HART

"Mad, sire? Ah, yes — mad indeed, but
observe how they do light up the sky."
Old Skroob in "The Idle Jeste."

★

★

DRAMATISTS
PLAY SERVICE
INC.

LIGHT UP THE SKY was first presented by Joseph M. Hyman and Bernard Hart at the Royale Theatre, New York City, on November 18, 1948, with the following cast:

(In order of appearance)

MISS LOWELL	Jane Middleton
CARLETON FITZGERALD	Glenn Anders
FRANCES BLACK	Audrey Christie
OWEN TURNER	Philip Ober
STELLA LIVINGSTON	Phyllis Povah
PETER SLOAN	Barry Nelson
SIDNEY BLACK	Sam Levene
SVEN	Si Oakland
IRENE LIVINGSTON	Virginia Field
TYLER RAYBURN	Bartlett Robinson
A SHRINER	John D. Seymour
WILLIAM H. GALLEGHER	Donald McClelland
A PLAIN-CLOTHES MAN	Ronald Alexander

Directed by Moss HART
Setting by FREDERIC FOX
Furs designed by MAXIMILIAN
Costumes Designed by KIVIETTE

SCENE

ACT I

The living-room of Irene Livingston's Ritz-Carlton Hotel suite at Boston, Mass. Time 5:30 P. M.

ACT II

The same. Time about 11:45 that evening.

ACT III

The same. Time 3:30 A. M.

3

LIGHT UP THE SKY

ACT I

Although it is almost five-thirty, MISS IRENE LIVINGSTON'S
*suite in Boston's Ritz-Carlton Hotel is wonderfully serene
and quiet this December afternoon, and the gentle calm
and discreet silence give the lie to those novels and stories
which always portray a famous lady of the stage in a
state bordering on hysteria as the hour approaches when
the curtain rises on the first performance, and depict her
suite as a shambles. Indeed, the only sign that would
mark this suite different from any other in the hotel is
the profusion of flowers and floral offerings in baskets,
all with cards attached, and a parrot in a cage in one
corner of the room. In an opposite corner, a trimly
tailored young lady,* NAN LOWELL, *sits in back of a
bridge table on which reposes a portable typewriter and
a great many sheets of paper on which she is quietly at
work.* MISS LOWELL *puzzles over what are obviously
handwritten scrawls on the yellow sheets of paper, pauses
for a moment or two to digest the contents, and then
types quickly and expertly on the machine. There is an
interval of silence as she finishes typing and picks up
another sheet of yellow paper to decipher—a silence
which is broken by the* PARROT *who speaks loudly and
distinctly from the other side of the room. For details on
the setting, see stage diagram on page 67.*

PARROT.* Oh, so you've got a parrot! (MISS LOWELL *looks toward
cage briefly, but goes right on with her work. In a moment, how-
ever,* PARROT *is loudly at it again.*) S. R. O., darling. (MISS LOWELL
stops typing.) S. R. O.! No seats till January. Bless you, darling!
(MISS LOWELL *looks up annoyed, and calls loudly across room:*

---

* When this play was produced in New York, a stuffed parrot was used and an
actor off-stage spoke through a microphone, thus giving a satisfactory effect to the
parrot's lines.

4

" *Sh-sh!* " *For a moment there is silence. Then:*) Think you're smart, don't you? Think you're George Jean Nathan! (*Exasperated,* MISS LOWELL *slams papers down on table, and strides across room to parrot cage which she promptly puts a cloth cover over. Then she goes back to table, and resumes her work. There is a knock at door.*)

MISS LOWELL. Come in.—Hello, Mr. Fitzgerald. (*Crosses down above* R. C. *chair.* CARLETON FITZGERALD *enters the room, or to be more accurate, he pervades it. There is no such thing as merely entering a room for* CARLETON FITZGERALD. *Any action, no matter how inconsequential, is filled with drama for him. Even his clothes have a certain dramatic value. The battered hat and old Mackintosh he wears at the moment are a fitting costume, should the situation warrant it, for either humble martyrdom or splendid but innately modest triumph. He stands leaning against the closed door, regarding* MISS LOWELL *for a full theatrical pause. Then he sighs heavily, and speaks in a low, hushed voice vibrant with drama.*)

CARLETON. Irene asleep?

MISS LOWELL. No, Mr. Fitzgerald. She's having a massage. (*He swings away from door, and tenderly lets his fingertips rest on a flower or two below piano. Hat on chair below piano. He crosses to bar, then to drum table. Then he smiles wistfully, sighs once again, and lets his hand fall heavily to his side.*)

CARLETON. Charming. Lovely. I could cry.

MISS LOWELL. I beg your pardon?

CARLETON. (*Softly.*) It's five-thirty.

MISS LOWELL. (*Uncertainly.*) Yes—just about.

CARLETON. (*Crossing down below* R. C. *chair.*) Five-thirty. (*He sinks dramatically into a chair, his legs sprawled out in front of him, and stares up at ceiling.*) Six-thirty. Seven-thirty. Eight-thirty. The footlights dim. The curtain rises. (*He sits up and pushes his hat far back on his head.*) These next three hours, Miss Lowell. I could cry.

MISS LOWELL. You mean—nerves?

CARLETON. (*So gently.*) No, no—not nerves. My wife calls it " magic time "—those few magic hours when the play belongs to the author—(*He gestures upstairs to ceiling.*) the director—(*He indicates himself.*) and the actress who brings it alive. (*He gestures toward bedroom. Then he sighs.*) They never come again.

MISS LOWELL. Not even when you open in New York?

CARLETON. (*Crossing* U. C.) No. Never then. That's the market

5

place—the fishwife hawking her wares. (*Crosses above* L. C. *chair.*) The magic only happens out of town, Miss Lowell—those three hours before the curtain rises for the first time. I'm sorry you couldn't come to the dress rehearsal last night.

MISS LOWELL. Miss Livingston said you didn't allow anybody in the theater.

CARLETON. (*Crossing* U. *to bar.*) That's what I mean. I'm sorry. Belasco taught me never to break a rule—no matter how silly. You're coming tonight, of course?

MISS LOWELL. I bought a ticket. I'm going to see what good that does.

CARLETON. (*Crossing above* L. *end sofa.*) Sit well back. This is a shattering and beautiful play, Miss Lowell. A play of majesty and nobility. I had to move back to the last row last night. I cried when I read it, I cried when I directed it, and last night the cast could hear me sobbing. (*Crosses* D. C.) I had to move back.

MISS LOWELL. I'm sitting in the balcony.

CARLETON. (*Softly, sitting* R. C. *chair.*) The balcony . . . ! (*He smiles sadly.*) I saw them all from the balcony, Miss Lowell—all the great ones. A little boy in St. Louis sat in the balcony every Saturday afternoon, his chin pressed hard against the rail, and cried. (*Going right on.*) He didn't know then, that little boy, that one day he would direct Irene Livingston, (*Points to her door.*) and walk across the (*Points out of window.*) Common in Boston on a December afternoon and look up and see his name come on in lights over a theater. (*Rises.*) Look around you in the balcony tonight, Miss Lowell. (*Crosses above* R. C. *chair.*) Perhaps another little boy will be sitting there with his chin pressed hard against the rail, his heart beating and his blood pounding with that first magic. (*Crosses* L. *to bar, looks out of window.*) That sign's not lit yet, Goddamit. Well, they're not going to save current while we're here. (*Phone rings. He starts angrily toward it.*) I think it's for me. I put a call in for my wife and told them I'd be here. Hello? Yes, this is he. Put the call through. Hello? Hello, Margaret. Oh, just wonderful, darling. Noble and wonderful. I could cry. No, line rehearsal at two and I let them go. I wanted Irene fresh for tonight. No, she's having a massage. (*He listens for a moment.*) What? No. No, I haven't walked across the Common yet. It's freezing and the damn sign isn't lit up yet. I was just going to call the theater. (*Crosses* D. *around* R. C. *chair and sits.*) Thank you, my darling. Can you feel the magic there, too? Of course! Darling, get out the scrap books—no, no, mine—not yours, and read those old first St. Louis notices. It would please me to know you were doing that. That foolish fellow is part of tonight, isn't he? Oh, Margaret, my dear, you're much too kind. Tremble a little for us, darling, and call me here, in Irene's room, about one. Good-bye, darling. (*Hangs up and looks at his watch. Rises, crosses* C.) Miss Lowell, would you do me a favor?

MISS LOWELL. Certainly, Mr. Fitzgerald.

CARLETON. Would you call the theater? Tell them to light up that sign, immediately—it's very bad luck, you know. And tell Irene I'll stop by. (*Crosses to* R. C. *chair.*) I have a talisman for her to wear tonight. (*He crosses to door and turns to her again, looks around room, gets hat from piano chair.*) Magic time! Feel it, Miss Lowell?

MISS LOWELL. Not exactly. This is all quite new to me, you know.

CARLETON. (*Crosses* D. *above* R. C. *chair.*) You will, my dear. Suddenly you'll want to cry. (*Crosses* U. *to door.*) You *will* phone those bastards, won't you?

MISS LOWELL. Yes. (*He smiles sweetly at her and closes door behind him.* MISS LOWELL *crosses to phone below sofa and picks up receiver.*) Will you get me the Colonial Theater, please? Thanks. (*While she waits, she looks idly out window. Suddenly she clicks phone.*) Never mind, operator. It's all right. (*She goes back to bridge table and picks up a pile of yellow sheets wrathfully. There is a knock at door.*) Come in. (FRANCES BLACK *comes into room, her face rosy, her arms full of packages, her vitality something fearful.*)

FRANCES. (*Crossing* D. *above* L. *chair, puts down hat box.*) Hi-ya, honey. I thought maybe Sidney was here. I called the room and the barber shop, but no dice, so I thought maybe he was up here. Where's everybody? Dead or something? (*Crosses to* R. C. *chair.*)

MISS LOWELL. Miss Livingston's having a massage.

FRANCES. Boy, I could stand somebody to pound my behind right now. I'm beat.

MISS LOWELL. Been shopping?

FRANCES. (*Sits* R. C. *chair.*) You said it, honey. If Sidney can sink three hundred thousand bucks into a play, I can shop—and when I say shop, honey, I ain't kidding. Get a load of that. (*She stretches out her hand, one finger bearing a huge topaz ring.*) I didn't have it when I went out, honey. And I got a little platina fox cape to wear to the opening tonight that's a real yummy.

7

Sidney'll drop dead, but so what? He buys Renoirs and Utrillos—I buy stuff to hang on myself—not the walls. Say, honey, is Stella around? We got a gin game to finish.

MISS LOWELL. She went out about an hour ago.

FRANCES. You know something, honey? That old bag plays a real gutsy game of gin. Yattata, yattata, yattata, all the time—she don't even hold her cards right—and then " boffo "—she slips it to you. Gin. (*Rises, crosses to above* L. *chair, picks up hat box.*) If she comes back, tell her I'm just parking this junk—maybe we can get in a fast game before dinner. (*Crosses* U. *to parrot cage.*) Hi-ya, kid. What do you hear from the mob? Huh, Happy Joe. (*Crosses to door.*)

MISS LOWELL. I'll tell her, Mrs. Black.

FRANCES. (*She stops at door. Crosses* D. C.) Say, honey, did *you* see the dress rehearsal last night?

MISS LOWELL. I wasn't allowed in, Mrs. Black.

FRANCES. Me too, honey. Some big deal. Huh. A guy puts up three hundred thousand bucks and his wife ain't allowed in the theater. It's gonna melt, or something, if somebody looks at it.

MISS LOWELL. I believe it's an unshakable rule of Mr. Fitzgerald's.

FRANCES. Oh, honey, is he kidding? Honest, I sit and listen to him sometimes with my mouth hanging open, and look around and everyone else is taking it deadpan, and Sidney, who's a mugg like me, is drinking it in and lapping it up and giving out with that " I could cry " routine, so that I think maybe *I'm* nuts. Don't get me wrong, Miss Lowell, my husband's a great guy—he's running in the long-haired derby tonight, and I don't want to see him get hurt. Well, honey, they gotta let the common people in for a gander tonight so we'll see. (*Crosses* U. *to door.*) Tell Stella I'll be right down. S'long. Say, it'll be a hell of a note if that curtain goes up and nobody cries but Mr. Fitzgerald. (*She goes out. With a sigh,* MISS LOWELL *goes to desk* R., *but not for long. Again there is a knock at door. This time* MISS LOWELL *puts down papers very carefully, folds her arms, and speaks almost cooingly.*)

MISS LOWELL. (*Crossing above sofa.*) Come in . . . (OWEN TURNER *comes into the room,* U. C. *A nice looking man in his late forties, quiet, soft-spoken, urbane.*)

OWEN. Am I too early?

MISS LOWELL. Too early?

8

OWEN. Miss Livingston asked me to come in for a good luck drink about five-thirty.

MISS LOWELL. Oh. She's having a massage. I'm sure she'll be out in a few moments. Please sit down. My name is Nan Lowell.

OWEN. (*Crossing* D. *to* L. C. *chair, and sitting in it.*) How-do-you-do. Mine's Owen Turner.

MISS LOWELL. (*Crossing* D. *to* C.) How-do-you-do. Well, well. I'm afraid I'm an old admirer of your plays, Mr. Turner.

OWEN. Why, thank you.

MISS LOWELL. I've even played in two or three of them.

OWEN. Did you? I don't seem to recall ——

MISS LOWELL. (*Laughingly.*) No, no. In college. I'm not an actress. I'm that repellent literary invention—a ghost writer. (*She gestures toward papers and typewriter.*) Miss Livingston's Autobiography.

OWEN. Oh, yes. I saw it announced for the fall.

MISS LOWELL. Spring publication, now—with luck. If her handwriting gets no worse and I can keep the more libelous portions out. By the way, I haven't come to *you* yet, Mr. Turner.

OWEN. I doubt if she'll include me, Miss Lowell.

MISS LOWELL. You did two plays together, didn't you?

OWEN. Yes, we did, but the author is always the least colorful figure in Irene's orbit. Is there a title yet? (*He indicates papers on table.*)

MISS LOWELL. (*Crossing to coffee table.*) As of ten minutes of six, yes. This is today's title. (*Crosses to* OWEN *with paper.*) We change it every day. (*She picks up a piece of paper.*)

OWEN. "With a Bow to the Moon." A suggestion of Mr. Fitzgerald's?

MISS LOWELL. How did you know?

OWEN. Scar tissue. He directed those two plays of mine.

MISS LOWELL. (*Smiling.*) He's quite an emotional man, isn't he?

OWEN. Indeed. He cries at card tricks.

MISS LOWELL. (*Crossing to sofa, puts paper down on coffee table, sits sofa.*) Is a new play of yours opening up here, Mr. Turner? Forgive my not knowing—I haven't even glanced at a paper this last week.

OWEN. No, I have no new play this year. Thank God.

MISS LOWELL. Oh? (*She looks at him questioningly, too polite to ask why.*)

OWEN. (*Rising and crossing to* R. C. *Smiling at her.*) Are you very

9

new to all this, Miss Lowell? (*His gesture takes in room, flowers, and all that it implies.*)

MISS LOWELL. Very. The literary world is my bailiwick.

OWEN. I'm afraid you wouldn't understand then. It's almost like trying to explain music to someone who was born deaf.

MISS LOWELL. That tough? (*Gently.*)

OWEN. (*Laughing.*) I didn't mean to sound quite so patronizing. There are certain refinements in the process of putting on a play that give the author more clean healthy pain than even the critics, I assure you. (*Crosses* U. *above* R. C. *chair.*) This is my sabbatical. This is my year of watching the pain of others, and not even thinking of my own, past or future. I can't describe what exquisite pleasure it gives me, Miss Lowell. After years of standing in back of the theater waiting for friends to come up the aisle and say, " It needs work, Owen," now I come up the aisle and say it. It's a delicious feeling. (*Crosses above to* R. *end of sofa.*)

MISS LOWELL. I gather you expect the worst tonight, Mr. Turner.

OWEN. No, not necessarily. Actually, I do wish them well. But if the worse should happen, I'm right on hand to enjoy it. Old playwrights never die, Miss Lowell—they just go out of town. (*Crosses* D., *sits* R. *end of sofa.*) Tell me, were you at the dress rehearsal last night?

MISS LOWELL. No, sir! Wasn't allowed in.

OWEN. Oh, yes, of course. I'd forgotten. That's when the magic time begins for Mr. Fitzgerald, isn't it?

MISS LOWELL. Yes. I believe it goes on until eight-thirty tonight—rather like a Jewish holiday.

OWEN. All but the fasting. He eats like a horse, you know, no matter what happens. By the way, is Miss Livingston's mother up here with her?

MISS LOWELL. Stella? Yes, indeed.

OWEN. Good. A breath of foul air in the middle of magic time. Who else is here, Miss Lowell? I'd enjoy knowing the full cast, if you don't mind.

MISS LOWELL. Well, Sidney Black, of course, and his wife Frances. Miss Livingston's husband arrives in time for dinner, and Mr. Fitzgerald, of course. That's the cast—complete.

OWEN. No, it isn't.

MISS LOWELL. Isn't it?

OWEN (*Rising and crossing below coffee table to* C.) No. As usual, at magic time, someone is always left out, and I hardly think it's pure accident that it's always the same one.

MISS LOWELL. (*Rising.*) Who, for goodness' sake? Who have I left out?

OWEN. (*Smiling.*) Just the author of this play, Miss Lowell. Quite a natural omission under the circumstances, I assure you. (*Crosses above* L. C. *chair.*)

MISS LOWELL. Good God! Magic time isn't catching, is it, Mr. Turner?

OWEN. No. What's he like? Quite young, I understand.

MISS LOWELL. (*Puts typewriter and papers on desk.*) Yes. And extremely nice. He's rather shy and not very talkative, but I wouldn't want to push him around. Can't I fix you a drink while you're waiting, Mr. Turner?

OWEN. Thank you, no. I wouldn't spoil Irene's entrance for anything. (*There is a raucous laugh outside door. They both turn.*) I shan't need one for a bit, anyway, Miss Lowell. That is unmistakably Stella. (*Crosses below drum table to* D. L. *And* STELLA *it is. She slams door behind her and plunges headlong toward* MISS LOWELL.)

STELLA. Tell them a joke and give 'em a good laugh and they like it better. I haven't tipped a bell-boy in twenty years, Miss Lowell. (*She deposits a large sheaf of telegrams and a copy of " Variety " on the door chair and starts to remove her coat.* STELLA *is almost a perfect specimen of that redoubtable old pirate and saboteur, the mother of the star. The veteran of a thousand fights and feuds from which she has invariably emerged unscarred, her age is as uncertain as the color of her hair, and as carefully guarded a secret. She is quite a handsome old hoodlum, and very well turned out, since most of* IRENE'S *furs and hats ultimately find a safe haven on* STELLA, *and she has retained, undaunted through the years, the spirit and ethics of a Dead End Kid. She becomes aware that* MISS LOWELL *is looking past her and turns. For a moment she peers nearsightedly across the room. Then:*) Owen? Is that Owen Turner? (*Crosses* D. C.)

OWEN. (*Crossing to* D. C.) As ever was, Stella. How are you? (*They shake hands.*)

STELLA. Why, Owen Turner! I was thinking about you just fifteen minutes ago! Don't tell me I'm not psychic! Not fifteen minutes ago I walked into the Ladies' Room downstairs and your name was on the tip of my tongue. What do you make of that!

11

OWEN. The connection escapes me for a moment, Stella.

STELLA. (*To* MISS LOWELL.) My slip was showing and I went into the Ladies' Room to fix it and while the matron was sewing the strap, I said to myself, "My God, I wish Irene were opening in a show by Owen Turner tonight." (*She turns to* MISS LOWELL.) Did you know he wrote two wonderful plays for Irene, dear?

MISS LOWELL. Yes, I did.

STELLA. Haven't got a new one up your sleeve for her, have you, Owen?

OWEN. (*Crossing* U. L.) No. No, Stella. No. (*He shakes his head.*)

STELLA. She's going to need one, dear. By eleven o'clock tonight, if you ask me. And I'll tell you something else —— (*She stops dead and looks at parrot cage.*) Who put the cover over Orson?

MISS LOWELL. I'm afraid I did, Mrs. Livingston. I was trying to work.

STELLA. Well, that settles it! Once before somebody put the cover over Orson on the day of an opening and we closed out of town in a week. (*Crosses* U. *to cage, opens cover.*)

MISS LOWELL. I'm very sorry, Miss Livingston. Nobody warned me.

STELLA. (*Crossing to door chair, takes off coat, puts on chair.*) Oh, it doesn't matter. Nothing can hurt *this* one. Just the curtain going up is enough.

OWEN. (*Crossing* D. *to* L. C. *chair, sits.*) Now, now, Stella. You always say that. You're always Cassandra the day of the opening. Besides, you haven't even seen it yet—which somewhat weakens your point.

STELLA. (*Crossing* D. *to* L. C.) Like hell I haven't seen it! I saw it till half-past twelve last night—then I came home and cut down my Christmas list and Irene's contribution to the Actors' Fund.

OWEN. Well, well! Mr. Fitzgerald let you in? What form of blackmail did you use, Stella? I'm interested.

STELLA. Listen, I wouldn't ask Carleton to let me into a paper bag. I got in myself and I saw and heard the whole thing, including that sonofabitch sobbing. Now don't you breathe one word of this. (*To* MISS LOWELL. *Crosses to sofa, motions* OWEN *to her.* OWEN *crosses to sofa, sits. She looks toward bedroom door and lowers her voice.*) I got up at seven o'clock in the morning yesterday and left a note for Irene saying I was going to Brookline for the day— to visit an old friend. Instead I went to the theater and went in with the cleaning women. I gave one of them five dollars to give me her clothes—and I stayed up in the balcony with a mop and pail and a rag around my hair. Saw the whole dress rehearsal. I damn near starved.

OWEN. You were hardly in the mood to enjoy the play, Stella.

STELLA. I wasn't, eh? Well, take a friend's advice and see this show on an empty stomach tonight, Owen. You know what it's about, don't you?

OWEN. No, I don't. And please don't tell me. Does Irene know you've seen it?

STELLA. I should say not. Nobody does. Why, Owen, I wasn't even allowed to *read* it. Nobody was. You never *saw* such carryings-on! Why, once I went to the theater to pick up Irene at rehearsal, and I damn near crossed myself. Everyone tiptoeing around, speaking in whispers—it was like going into a cathedral. Irene takes my hand and says: " It may be, Mother, that after this beautiful play, I shall never act again." (*Takes* OWEN'S *hand.*) And everyone kind of lowered their heads as if they were praying. Well, it may be that I'm crazy, but it may also be that this is the biggest bunch of crap ever put on any stage. How about a drink?

OWEN. No, thanks, Stella.

STELLA. (*Rising, crosses below coffee table, u. to bar, pours drink.*) I'm never going to see this play sober again, that's one thing I'm sure of. (*She starts across to bar. There is a knock at door.*) Come in. Oh, hello. (*Crosses* D. R. C. PETER SLOAN *comes into the room. He is in his middle thirties, with the body and face of a good-humored longshoreman, and the brooding deep-set eyes of a poet. His manner is diffident and shy, and he stands for a moment in doorway, smiling at* STELLA *and* MISS LOWELL.)

PETER. Irene asked me to come up for a good luck drink.

STELLA. (*Crossing to* PETER.) Sure. Come on in. She'll be right out. I was just having a good luck drink myself and telling Mr. Turner how wonderful everyone says your play is. That is, those who have seen it—like the actors and Mr. Fitzgerald. This is the young man that did it, Owen. (*Crosses to above drum table.*)

OWEN. (*Rising.*) How-do-you-do.

PETER. Hello. Peter Sloan is the name.

STELLA. (*Crossing to* PETER.) Oh, excuse me. You know me and names. (OWEN *sits on sofa.*) Well, I'm sure they'll all know your name tomorrow, Mr. Sloan. Never heard such wonderful things about a play. Seems a pity to open it—everyone's enjoyed re-

13

hearsals so. Well, I'm going to take my good luck drink inside and get dressed, if you don't mind. (*Crosses to door* D. L.) I can wish just as hard in there—harder! (*She smiles brightly at them all and goes into her room, directly opposite* IRENE'S. *There is a little silence after she goes.* PETER *sits down* R. C. *in a chair, but says nothing. Finally:*)

OWEN. Is this your first play, Mr. Sloan?

PETER. Yes.

OWEN. Well, that's quite an occasion.

PETER. Thanks. (*Silence again.* OWEN *looks at* MISS LOWELL, *who shrugs. Then:*)

OWEN. The play is opening tonight? You're sure of it?

PETER. What? Oh, yes. Yes, of course. Why?

OWEN. As an old practitioner myself, you seem to me extraordinarily calm.

PETER. (*Smiling.*) Oh. No . . . I've got an upset stomach. And I've been sick as a dog for two days.

MISS LOWELL. I thought I hadn't seen you around. What are you doing for it?

PETER. Acting surprised, mostly. (*He laughs ruefully.*) When I was driving a truck my stomach was fine. You figure it out. I used to drive the night run between Omaha and Chicago and eat in every two-bit hash joint on the route and my stomach was fine. Now I'm glad if farina stays down.

OWEN. Good. Always glad to welcome a new member of the Dramatists' Guild. But that's an interesting leap, Mr. Sloan—from the truck to the typewriter. How did you manage it?

PETER. I dunno. Only way I could afford to write. It's a two-day drive to Chicago and then you get two days off. I slept one whole day, and then I had all the next day free to work.

OWEN. That's certainly getting into our union the hard way.

PETER. (*Laughing.*) Well, it's not as tough as it sounds. I wound up soda-jerking and dish-washing before I finished the damn play. Trucking was easy.

OWEN. (*Rising and crossing to above* L. C. *chair.*) Well, I shall certainly avoid all those Sunday stories about you after the play opens, Mr. Sloan. You're much too colorful a figure. But I'm more eager now than ever to see that play tonight.

PETER. (*Rising and crossing* U. C.) Thanks. As far as I'm concerned, it's all velvet right now. I never expected to see this play

14

in front of an audience, anyway. Not in a million years.

OWEN. Why not?

PETER. (*Shrugging his shoulders.*) I wrote it to get a lot of things off my chest—kind of a personal crusade. I never thought anyone would do it, and I didn't give a damn. I wanted it on paper. The big kick for me, no matter what happens tonight, is the humanity of these people. (*Crosses above sofa.*)

MISS LOWELL. What people?

PETER. All of them. Miss Livingston, Sidney Black, Fitzgerald—all of 'em. I've been banging around since I was a kid of twelve, and it's nice, once in a while, to meet up with a bunch of people doing something with their hearts instead of their heads or their pocketbooks. It's a damn nice thing to see.

OWEN. (*Crossing D. sits L. C. chair.*) Indeed—though I'm not quite sure I understand what you mean.

PETER. (*Crossing C. to OWEN.*) I mean—here they are—all of 'em —working like horses, pouring out money, staking their reputations, pushing aside all thoughts of personal gain and self-interest —why? For what? They like this play of mine—but that's not the whole answer. Irene's playing an old woman of seventy and doesn't speak a line for the whole first act. Fitzgerald postponed his wife's play and paid off the cast to get this on right away. Sidney Black planked down three hundred thousand dollars. That's more than just liking or believing in a play, for my money, Mr. Turner. It's deeper than that. (*Crosses D. below R. C. chair.*) These people are good in heart—they have the wonderful courage of dreamers and fools. And there's not too much of that around. (*He stops, startled.*) My God, an upset stomach makes you talk a lot! (*Sits R. C. chair.*)

OWEN. (*Rising and crossing U. L. to window.*) Not for a minute, Mr. Sloan, not for a minute. And how I shall contain myself until eight-thirty tonight, I don't know. (*There is a knock at the door, but this time door is opened without waiting for an invitation to come in, and SIDNEY BLACK stands in doorway. He is a short man in a dark blue suit with a dark blue tie and hat, but this dark blue façade, from which he never varies, conceals a blazing dynamo of lightning blue sparks beneath. He is a "one purpose guy" as he would say himself, and he has done extremely well in the "one purpose" department. At the age of forty-two, he is a solid millionaire, and though the project and the method of accumulation have sometimes wavered dangerously close to the knuckle,*

SIDNEY BLACK *and his " one purpose" haven't. That purpose was always money, that's what* SIDNEY *has plenty of, and that's what he intends to keep and make more of, his big new discovery being that there is money in paintings, in antique silver and furniture, and very possibly in literature and the theater. It has given new zest to his savage acquisitiveness. He comes quickly into the room, waving a " hello" to* PETER *and* MISS LOWELL.)

SIDNEY. (*Crossing to* MISS LOWELL *above sofa.*) Weather clear, track fast, the flag is up. Where is our lovely lady? I found this Georgian silver baptismal cup I would like to place in her hands. Where is she, Miss Lowell?

MISS LOWELL. She's having a massage, Mr. Black.

SIDNEY. Good. The heavy honey-dew of slumber before an opening. Peter, my dear boy, this night. Owen! (*Crosses to meet* OWEN *at* C.) Nobody told me you were in Boston. Well! This begins to look like what Frances calls a very stylish affair. Glad to see you. (*He inclines his head toward* PETER *as they shake hands.*) Did I interrupt you two fellows who make with the words? Go right ahead. (*Crosses* U. *to love-seat, puts down package and coat.*) Me, I'm just a crepe paper moon over the Taj Mahal, waiting for Scheherazade to start the entertainment. I always listen when Toscanini gives the downbeat. Go right ahead.

OWEN. (*Sits* L. C. *chair.*) I think you came in on Deems Taylor, Sidney—we're all finished. But Mr. Sloan has me practically panting for the curtain to go up tonight.

SIDNEY. You mean our tattered Tolstoy has been talking, Owen? (*Crosses* D. *above sofa.*) Why, that's like picking diamonds out of the herring at Lindy's. (*Sits sofa* C.) What did I miss, Peter?

PETER. Nothing.

SIDNEY. You see? I'm lucky to get a two-syllable word. (*Crosses above* PETER.) Here's a fellow who takes a yellow sheet of paper, Owen, and makes it sing like a first folio—you try and talk to him and he makes the doorman downstairs sound like Bernard Shaw drinking vodka instead of vegetable juice. (*Crosses* C.) Now, Mr. Turner talks like a playwright, Peter. You put a nickel in the slot and out comes playwright talk. This I understand. (*Crosses to bar, gets bottle and shot glass.*) This is my type playwright.

OWEN. (*Laughing.*) That's not what the audience cares about, Sidney.

SIDNEY. (*Crossing* D. L., *leans on back of* L. *chair.*) I'm only kid-

16

ding. This is our big private joke. (*Crosses* D. L.) When I went to meet Peter for the first time after I read the play, I said to Frances: "How do you say hello to the Salzburg Festival? How do you shake hands with Tchaikowsky's Fifth?" Then I meet our tonguetied friend and I realize I'm talking to Coolidge with a head cold. I finally had to turn to Irene and say: "You're sure this is the fellow who wrote it?" Remember, Peter?

PETER. Yes.

SIDNEY. See, Owen? We're right back to the one-syllable words.

OWEN. Irene sent you the play?

SIDNEY. She didn't send it to me—she brought it to me—like Joan of Arc bringing the King the crown and a hot corned-beef sandwich. And both bad bets. Owen, I'm a guy who parts very slowly from a buck.

OWEN. I've heard tell.

SIDNEY. When I let go that eagle not only screams—it goes back to the mint with a double rupture. What's more, I'm all set once again to invade most of the forty-eight States with my Ice Show. This is a razzamatazz I know from Owen. A sweet and sure annuity—it's like taking a bath at Fort Knox. I know when I put Frances on her skates and let the fans see her spangled panties swinging low against the ice while that orchestra plays " I Wonder Who's Kissing Her Now" (*Crosses* U. *to bar, puts down bottle and glass*), I'm good for at least a Cezanne and maybe a Matisse and we're not going to eat rye bread in the country this summer, either. (*Crosses* C.) What do I need with the theater—a cockamamie business where you get one roll of the dice from seven middle-aged men on the aisle who hated Mickey Mouse when they were kids. I need them like a hole in the head. So what happens? I read the play, I write out a check for three hundred thousand dollars, and Frances keeps her can warm this winter. That's what Silent Sam here does to a smart money boy—(*Crosses to* PETER.) just by putting wonderful words together on a piece of paper. And to give it the real, corny, technicolor schmaltz, me, the sucker, I'm happy. I don't regret one dollar of it. You happy, too, Peter? Like what we've done with your baby?

PETER. Yes. Very.

SIDNEY. He must be. Two words. (*Crosses above sofa to* D. R.) Well, in a little while we'll take the curtain up, Peter, and give Mr. Turner and Miss Lowell a look, eh? We're sticking a Roman Candle into the tired face of show business tonight, Owen, and

17

the sparks that fly are going to light up the theater like an old-fashioned Fourth of July. (*Crosses below sofa.*) Me, I'm only the guy who paid for the ink on the Declaration of Independence— I just lurk in the light of the rockets' red glare—but I'm proud to have standing room. Signed, Sidney Black. (*Sits sofa.*) Say, it's a quarter of six! Shouldn't somebody wake up Irene? At a quarter to —— (MISS LOWELL *starts to rise, but as she does so, door of* IRENE'S *room opens, and* SVEN, *the masseur, carrying a little black bag and a massage table, comes out.*)

SVEN. Good evening. (*He crosses room without another word and goes out* C., *as others rise, awaiting* IRENE'S *entrance.* OWEN *crosses* U. *to bar.*)

SIDNEY. Good evening. (*In a moment* IRENE *appears, a whirl of chiffon negligee—exuding that ineffable essence of a great star of the stage. For an instant she stands poised in the doorway, blinking her eyes, as if to get the sleep out of them—then suddenly she covers her face with her hands and begins to sob.*)

IRENE. Bless you, my darlings.

SIDNEY. Irene!! (SIDNEY *crosses* U. *to her* R. PETER *crosses* U. *to her* L.)

MISS LOWELL. Help her to a chair, I'll get some brandy. (*Crosses* U. *to bar.*)

IRENE. (*Through her sobs.*) Forgive me, please! I'm so sorry! Forgive me!

SIDNEY. Irene! What is it? What's the matter?

PETER. What's happened? (*They help her down to* R. C. *chair,* SIDNEY *at her* L., PETER *above phone table.*)

IRENE. I'm so sorry—so very sorry. (*They start down.* PETER *and* SIDNEY *rush to her side, while* MISS LOWELL *rushes to get brandy. They help her tenderly toward chair,* R. C. *Still sobbing, and as she passes* OWEN, *she removes her hands from her tear-stained face long enough to toss him a choked:*) Owen, darling! (*They kneel on each side of her,* MISS LOWELL *crosses back to* IRENE *ready with glass of liquor.*)

SIDNEY. What is it, Irene—what's the matter?

PETER. Shall we get a doctor?

MISS LOWELL. (*Below them, at her* R., *kneeling.*) Try and drink this, Miss Livingston—it may help! (OWEN *crosses* D. *above drum table.*)

IRENE. No, no—please—I—I'm such a fool! It's so stupid to do this—I can't help it—I can't.—Forgive me, Sidney. Peter!

18

SIDNEY. (*At* L.) But what *is* it, Irene? Are you sick? Are we going to open tonight! What is it?

IRENE. Oh, darling, darling! I'm so sorry to do this!

PETER. Maybe we can help, if you'll only tell us, Irene.

IRENE. Peter, darling! I've upset you—I've upset you all!

SIDNEY. To hell with upsetting us! It's *you* we're worried about! For God's sake, what is it!

IRENE. Oh, Sidney, don't—don't make me think of it! It's all so —— (*She covers her face with her hands again.*)

SIDNEY. What'll we do? (*Takes step* U. C. *A quick look at his watch.*) We better do *something!*

OWEN. (*Steps* L. C.) Sidney, I think if you would all just move upstage—I mean, if you would all just clear away for a moment, and let Irene, that is, if you would just let her be quite quiet for a moment or two, I'm sure she'll be able to tell you. (SIDNEY *crossses* U. *to bar,* PETER *crosses* U. *below alcove,* MISS LOWELL *crosses to desk* D. R. *They move away from chair and stand waiting anxiously behind her. In a moment, the sobbing stops and she wipes her eyes and blows her nose. Then, with a great shiver of the shoulders as if finally regaining complete control, she speaks:*)

IRENE. Peter—Sidney—give me your hand—each of you. (*They cross to her, she takes their hands.*) Promise me you'll forgive me for upsetting you like this?

SIDNEY. You're forgiven right now! It's *you* we're worried about. Now are you all right for tonight?

IRENE. Oh, darling, of course! (*Rises and crosses to* SIDNEY.) Do you think anything short of death itself could stop me from going on in Peter's beautiful play? (*Crosses to* OWEN.) And, Owen darling, come and kiss me! How good of you to be here and how wonderful it is to see you! Give me a kiss, darling! I deserve a kiss. I'm saying such lovely things about you in my book! (OWEN *kisses her.*)

SIDNEY. Wait a minute. I thought you were going to tell us what was the matter, Irene?

IRENE. Matter? Oh, darling—it's gone! Completely gone! Isn't that wonderful! (IRENE *sits with* SIDNEY *on arm of* R. C. *chair.*) Now I can tell you! It was a nightmare—the most wretched, horrible nightmare! (*Turns to* OWEN.) I must have dozed off to sleep during the massage, and do you know what I dreamt? Well, it won't make any sense to you at all, unless —— (*Turns to* SIDNEY.) Shall we tell him? Oh, of course! Darling, I don't speak a line for

19

the entire first act—not a syllable! That's one of our surprises! Isn't it staggering?

OWEN. (*Quietly.*) It's historical!

IRENE. Bless you, darling. Well, my dears, suddenly I was dreaming that I was on the stage and the curtain was going up. Everything was exactly as it is—absolutely real. And then I began to speak. I took the lines from all the other actors and nobody spoke but me. I couldn't stop, it was horrible. (*Crosses* U. *to door* C.)

OWEN. (*Facing front.*) What a really great man Freud was!

IRENE. What was that, dear? (*Crosses* D. C.)

OWEN. Just muttering. Was that the end of it?

IRENE. Oh, no, darling. It went on and on as those awful nightmares do. And Peter (*Crosses to* PETER *above sofa.*) stood there weeping because I had ruined his beautiful play. And I was weeping, too, but I couldn't stop.

SIDNEY. (*Rise.*) Where was I? For three hundred thousand dollars I should at least be in there *some place.*

IRENE. Sidney, darling, (*Crosses to* SIDNEY.) you *were.* You were, indeed. You were chasing me with a pair of ice skates. (*She goes to bar.*) And your drinks! Your good-luck drinks! Whatever am I thinking of! Bless you, darlings, for waiting! Owen, dear, (SIDNEY *sits* R. C. *chair.*) I want to hear what you've been up to, and what you're writing, and how long you'll be here. (*Gives* OWEN *drink.*) We're all finished now with me and my silly dreams. Come ahead, darling, it will take our minds off the opening. (*Crosses* U. *to bar.*)

OWEN. I'm still mulling over the fact that you don't speak a line for the first act. What do you do, my dear—bark?

IRENE. (*Laughing, crosses above sofa to* PETER *with two drinks—* PETER *gives one to* MISS LOWELL.) Bless you, darling—you see, Peter, he doesn't believe it! He doesn't believe a thing like this is possible! Do you, Owen? Of course you don't! Why should you? Oh, I've been a bad girl at times, Peter—selfish and hoggish and difficult—Miss Lowell can. tell you, too—I haven't spared myself in the book, have I? But this is a new Irene, Owen. Sidney, have I been good? Sidney, tell him!

SIDNEY. Like a reformed whore at a Strawberry Festival. (*On laugh.* OWEN *sits* L. C. *chair,* PETER *crosses* D., *sits* R. *end sofa.*)

IRENE. (*Crossing* U. *to bar.*) Oh, bless you, bless you, darling! You see (C.), Owen? And it's Peter! Peter and his beautiful play. Here are the drinks. We mustn't (*Crosses to sofa, sits.*) toast until everyone gets here—it's bad luck, you know. Oh, my dears, how lovely this is—to be sitting here two hours before the opening—without frayed nerves—just humble and grateful for the privilege of going into my dressing room tonight. Sidney, dear, you're still looking upset! It was a dream, dear—a silly little nightmare. Don't worry, darling. Please!

SIDNEY. (*Rising and crossing* C.) I'm not worried. I was having a dream about your dream. How I watched you take the lines from all the other actors, then I climbed over the footlights and hit you over the head with a coca cola bottle.

IRENE. (*Laughing, rising and crossing* C. *to* SIDNEY.) My dear, I believe he'd do it! He'd kill anybody who hurt this beautiful play.

SIDNEY. I would.

IRENE. (*Crossing above sofa,* SIDNEY *crossing* U. *to bar.*) So would I. Peter, you've done something to all of us with your play. I think we should toast Peter while we're waiting. Come, it's bad luck if you don't toast the play. A toast for Peter!

SIDNEY. To Peter. (*But as they lift their glasses, outside door is thrown open by* FRANCES.)

FRANCES. (*Crossing* D. C.) Hello, kids. Give a look at the war paint! (*She stands in doorway, waiting to be admired, and if you like diamonds and platina fox, she is certainly worthy of admiration, for she is literally covered with both.*) They're gonna know there's an opening up here tonight—and it ain't a grocery store, either. Well, how are you, Owen! Who dug you up? (*Crosses* U. *to door* C.)

IRENE. Darling, you look divine! You're positively blinding! (*Crosses* U. *in alcove, opens wires.*)

SIDNEY. Baby, it's an opening—not a coronation! You don't have to put *everything* on.

FRANCES. Everything? I got enough left over for a complete change during intermission. You losing your memory or something? (*Crosses* D. *to* R. C. *chair, sits.*) Fix me a drink, snoogie. I want to toast Shakespeare, too. You nervous tonight, Shakesy? Say, Daddy, get a load of the topaze! In case you ever want to choke a horse, I can help you.

SIDNEY. (*Crossing* D. *above* R. C. *chair, gives* FRANCES *drink.*) My wife moves into a store like the Soviets into occupied territory. She dismantles it and sends it home bit by bit. But you're (*He kisses her fondly.*) wonderful, cookie. You wear (*Crosses above phone table.*) anything you want to! You wouldn't believe, would you, that this same dame gets down on her knees and scrubs floors? Cooks like Escoffier on wheels and always looks like a barrel full of stardust. (SIDNEY *kisses* FRANCES.)

FRANCES. Now, doll, don't get oogalie-googalie in front of people! I'm gonna blush! (STELLA *enters* D. L., *crossing below drum table*.)

IRENE. Why, Mother! (STELLA *has appeared in doorway of her bedroom, dressed for the opening, too, and while she lacks the blinding glitter of* FRANCES, *she is no mean figure in her own way*.) My dear, do you think anyone will look at poor little me on the stage at *all*?

STELLA. (*Crossing below to* C.) With a little luck—no!

FRANCES. (*Rising and crossing to* STELLA *at* C.) Well, get a load of Stella, will you! Honey, we're gonna walk down the aisle together and really give 'em their lumps! Come on, Peachy, (*Crosses to above* L. C. *chair,* STELLA *crosses above drum table to* L. *chair, they sit*) we got a game to finish.—Owen, will you park it over there?

OWEN. Anything to oblige. (*Crosses below to sofa, sits* R. *end*.)

FRANCES. She's beating my brains out.

IRENE. Mother, really, (*Crosses above drum table*.) you're not going to play that dreadful gin game *now*?

STELLA. Just playing off the last game, dear—I've got her on a schnide.

SIDNEY. You know, if ever the Bomb falls, I can just hear Frances saying: "Here it comes, kid—gin!" (*There is a knock at door*.)

IRENE. Come in. (CARLETON *enters, crosses* U. *on step of alcove*.) Bless you, darling, you're just in time! Now, we can have our toast.

CARLETON. Irene—before you propose our toast, I have a little presentation I should like to make. It belongs more properly to that moment just before they call: "Places, please!" but perhaps you should have it now.

IRENE. Oh, my darling.

CARLETON. Yes, I think you should have it now. (*Slowly, he comes right to her, and places* R. C. *chair at* C., *motions* IRENE *to sit. She does, putting his hand in his pocket, he brings forth a tissue paper package, carefully wrapped, which he holds aloft. Crosses to* IRENE'S L. *As they rise*.) No, not yet. Inside this paper, Irene, are some little glass beads—a little peasant necklace—but these tiny bits of glass glow with the light of immortality, for this great lady wore them, too, on the night of an opening. I give them to you

22

now—another great lady of the theater. I give you the necklace of Eleanora Duse. (*Hands her package.*)

IRENE. Oh, Carleton, no! No! Not Duse!

CARLETON. Yes, Irene. Duse's necklace!

IRENE. Oh, darling, it's too much! Duse! She wore them. She touched them! Oh, Carleton, my cup runneth over! I can't open it, darling. My hands are trembling! (*He opens package for her, and reverently places necklace over her head.*)

CARLETON. (*At C.*) Some day, my dear, on some far-off opening night, perhaps another great lady will wear this talisman, and it may be that they will call it not Duse's, but Irene Livingston's necklace.

IRENE. (*Rising.*) Oh, Carleton, darling, bless you, bless you. I'm going to cry.

CARLETON. So am I, my dear, so am I! (*They embrace, both weeping. CARLETON crosses U. C.*)

IRENE. (*Crosses to L. C. chair.*) Mother, look! The necklace Duse wore on an opening night!

STELLA. (*Looking up.*) How long did the show run, dear?

IRENE. Aren't they dreadful—not an ounce of sentiment! (*Crosses U. to bar, gets drink, gives it to CARLETON.*) Carleton, darling—a toast! You do it so beautifully! Come, darling! A toast!

CARLETON. (*So modest.*) No, no, my dear! I must not be the first. I merely pluck the strings of the harp—you and Peter make the music. You propose the toast, Irene—we'll all follow. (*Crosses above drum table.*)

IRENE. (*At C.*) First, I want to make a special toast to Owen! Owen—won't you say a few words? We are old co-workers, Owen and I. We've toasted together before. Darling, won't you give us your blessing?

OWEN. (*Rising.*) Gladly, Irene. Though my personal blessing seems singularly unnecessary. Not since the Atlantic Charter was drawn up have I felt such unselfish purpose and resolve. Success to you all. (*Sits.*)

IRENE. Bless you, darling.

SIDNEY. Spoken like a playwright. (*SIDNEY is two steps above phone table.*)

IRENE. (*Crossing U. to door, goes D. C.*) My dear friends, my toast is to Peter. I don't think you can ever know, Peter, dear, how much your play has meant to all of us. It has given us a chance to recapture that wonderful feeling that the theater is more than just make-believe—it has given us a chance to say what is in all of our hearts. I am forever grateful, darling, and I toast your triumph. (*Murmur of applause.*)

SIDNEY. Peter, my close-mouthed friend—you're trapped; about six words are indicated.

IRENE. Yes, yes, Peter! A toast from Peter! Come, darling—author, author!

CARLETON and SIDNEY. Author, author!

PETER. (*Miserably.*) Couldn't I write you all a letter?

IRENE. No, no, darling—you mustn't break the chain, (*Takes his arm, brings him* C.) it's bad luck.

SIDNEY. (*Crossing* D. *above* C. *of sofa.*) Try a few words, Peter. It's like olives. They taste better after the first one. Come on, Peter.

IRENE. Shh! Peter's going to speak!

PETER. (*A deep breath, then he plunges—at* C.) I used to think that actors were just people who liked to put make-up on their faces every night. That producers, directors, and all the rest were part of the whole absurd foolishness and vanity. I was wrong. If there's a debt owed, it's my debt to you—to all of you—for showing me a new world—a new frontier—the real democracy of the theater. Thank you for that. (*Applause.*)

IRENE. Bravo, Peter, bravo! That was beautiful.

PETER. Would you drink a toast with me to my girl?

IRENE. Of course.

PETER. She's not here tonight, but she's as much a part of this play as I am. She's suffered through every line of the play with me for two solid years. I don't think I'd have ever finished it without her. She's waited a long time for this and I know she's looking at the clock right now.—So—to Helen!

SIDNEY and IRENE. To Helen!

CARLETON. (PETER *crosses to sofa, sits.*) I could cry. (*Knock comes at door.*)

IRENE. Oh, damn! Come in! (TYLER RAYBURN, *carrying his bag, stands smiling in doorway.*)

TYLER. Hello, everybody! All ready to open? (*At* U. C.)

OWEN. Greetings, Tyler.

IRENE. Oh, Tyler, dear, (*Crosses* U. *to* TYLER.) you *do* always manage to break into things. You all know Tyler Rayburn, don't you—my husband? Darling, put your bags down, and fix yourself a drink. Hurry, darling—we're toasting the play and it's very bad

24

luck to break the chain. (TYLER *puts bag down* R. *of door and crosses to bar, gets drink, crosses above sofa.*)

SIDNEY. Irene, can a guy who loves the Chase National Bank like a brother say a few words?

IRENE. (*As* SIDNEY *crosses to* IRENE C.) Darling, none of this would have been possible without you. We owe this very moment to your generosity and your great heart, Sidney. Bless you, darling, always, for that. Of course you must speak.

SIDNEY. Irene—I don't know from words like generosity and great heart. With me generosity is something my relatives expect every Saturday night, and Great Heart is the name of a very good dog food. When a guy coughs up three hundred thousand dollars for a show, he doesn't deserve any thanks—he should run, not walk, to the nearest psychiatrist. So unless I'm nutty as a fruit cake, why do I do it? I'll tell you. Because when I read the play I forgot about money, and being a smart operator, and all the cute tricks I know: I only knew I had to see this play get on a stage, to be part of getting it on, and for the first time in my life, Mammy's little baby loves cancelled checks. . . . Prosit!

IRENE. Oh, Sidney, dear, that was just lovely. Touching and kind and warm. Bless you, darling.

TYLER. (CARLETON *crosses in to* C.) Very nice, very well said.

IRENE. (*Crossing* D. *to* R. C. *chair, sits.*) I do think a toast before an opening makes everything so much better. Takes away nerves and jitters and that dreadful feeling in the pit of the stomach. Don't we all feel better now, h'mm? (*There is a loud, intensely annoyed clearing of the throat from* CARLETON.) Oh, my God, how could I? (*Rises.*) Carleton's toast! Only the most important toast, that's all I forgot. Only the one we're all waiting for.

CARLETON. (*Crossing* U. L. *With icy sweetness.*) No, no. It's not important. Everything's been said quite adequately. I'm sure we all feel warm and cozy without me.

IRENE. (*Crossing* U. *to* CARLETON.) Darling, do you think I would open tonight without your toast? Oh, please, my dear, do forgive me! It was Tyler bursting in in the middle of everything that made me —— (*Crosses to* TYLER.) Really, Tyler, I do think that with all the trains running out of Grand Central Station you might find one that doesn't dump you into the Ritz at a perfectly ridiculous moment. (*Crosses back to* SIDNEY C.) Oh, darling, please. I shall be so upset! Sidney, make him.

SIDNEY. (*Crossing* U. *and bringing* CARLETON U. C.) Come on,

25

Carleton—it is even better this way. Yours is the bell on the wedding cake—the angel on top of the Christmas tree. (*Crosses back of* L. *chair*.) Come on! Glasses high, everybody!

IRENE. Carleton's toast, always the best toast, my darlings, Carleton's toast! (*There is a little moment of silence as* CARLETON *waits for all eyes to turn his way. Then:*)

CARLETON. (*Crossing* D. C.) Mine is not a toast—not a toast to ourselves. It is, instead, a grateful bow to a little old lady—a little old lady unknown to me—unknown to any of us—but who will be forever enshrined in my memory. Last night, during the dress rehearsal, there came a moment when I could no longer look at the stage. My eyes, I am not ashamed to admit, were dim with tears. I rose from my seat and walked up the aisle to the back of the theater, and, as I did so, I saw a shadowy figure in the balcony. I was about to stop the rehearsal and have the intruder put out when I looked again, and discovered it was a scrubwoman (STELLA *reacts.*)—a scrubwoman who had stayed behind after the others had gone, her own work not finished, and then the play had started, and she had been caught up in it. I watched her—she did not see me—her eyes were glued to the stage. There she stood, a shapeless, dirty, old harridan ——

STELLA. Oh! (*Reaction.*)

IRENE. Shhh, Mother, please!

CARLETON. —her face ravaged by time, her greasy hair stringing out from the rag tied around her head. My own eyes were too clouded to see her face clearly, but suddenly I knew that this withered crone, this hapless bag of bones, had discovered beauty. For in her trembling hands she held a mop—and she was tearing it to bits with emotion. So it is not to us that I raise this toast— but to her! To an unknown and unforgettable bit of human wreckage, who found beauty and a moment of rapture in our play. (*He raises his glass.*)

STELLA. (*Wrathfully.*) Gin, goddammit to hell, gin! (*Curtain begins to fall. And as the others raise their glasses, curtain falls.*)

IRENE. (*Just before curtain is down.*) Oh, bless you, darling, bless you!

CURTAIN

ACT II

TIME: *About 11:45 that evening.*

SCENE: *The same. Only one lamp is lit, and the stage is quiet for a few moments. Then the door opens, and* STELLA *and* FRANCES *are outlined in the light from the corridor.* STELLA *snaps on light and closes door behind her.* FRANCES *crosses* D. C., *takes off cape, shakes it, crosses to desk chair, puts fur over back of it, crosses to sofa, sits. Without a word,* STELLA *goes directly to bar and mixes two drinks and, still silent, comes over and hands one to* FRANCES. *Then she, too, sinks into a sofa, and in absolute silence they sip their drinks. Suddenly* PARROT *speaks.*

THE PARROT. S. R. O., darling, S. R. O. Bless you, darling! No seats 'til January!

STELLA. (*Looking across room.*) You should live so long. (*Raises her glass.*) Cheer up, Frances. It's only money. Sidney's lucky— you've still got your ice-skates. (*Takes another sip.*) Maybe that's where this play belongs—on ice.

FRANCES. (R.) It would still stink. (*Rises, crosses* U. *around* R. *end of sofa to* U. C.) There ain't enough ice in the world for what we saw tonight, Stella, believe me! (*She bangs her glass down on table and paces for a moment or two.*) One hundred and fifty thousand bucks! Do you realize how many times I have to fan my tail around an ice-rink for that kind of dough, Stella? (*Crosses to* C. *chair.*)

STELLA. It cost three hundred thousand, dear.

FRANCES. (*Crossing to table.*) I know damn well it did. Half of it's my dough. (*Crosses above* L. C. *chair.*)

STELLA. No kidding! I didn't know that.

FRANCES. It's true. Meet Mrs. Shmoe.

STELLA. Well, whaddeye know! What made you do it, Frances? (FRANCES *crosses* U. C.) I always figured you for a smart girl. You didn't read it, did you?

FRANCES. Who reads? (*Crosses* U. L., *crosses above* C. *of sofa.*) No—it wasn't that, Stella.

27

STELLA. What, then? (FRANCES *crosses* U. R. *above sofa.*) Sidney certainly didn't need *your* money, did he?

FRANCES. No. It was me. I begged him. I did it all by myself. Little Red Poppyhood.

STELLA. *Why*, for God's sake?

FRANCES. Why? (*Crosses around sofa* R.) He's been driving me crazy for years, that's why! Every jerk thing he does turns out all right. And I'm always the schnook. (*Sits.*) First it was antique silver. He'd disappear in the afternoon and the next morning a truck would drive up and unload. Soup tureens you could take a bath in, and meat platters they must have used to serve a whole cow. Georgian or Louie or DiMaggio for all I know. Cost thousands! Thousands! I hollered my head off. Said he was nuts, and being played for a sucker, but he says it was an investment in the world's culture, so after a while I quit hollering—figuring culture I know about—that drives up in a truck—is better than some dame I don't know about—that drives around in a Cadillac. So what happens? In two years the stuff is worth twice. Maybe three times what he paid for it. (*Rises, crosses* D. R.) That's number one.

STELLA. But what has that got to do with ——?

FRANCES. (*Crossing below coffee table to* D. C.) Next it's pictures. (*Crosses* R. C.) Old Masters he starts coming home with. You ought to see 'em. Old Masters—Old Bastards! We got two in the bedroom. Scare the hell out of you. I wake up in the morning and (*Crossing* C.) feel my way around with my eyes tight shut. (*Crosses to* R. C. *chair, sits.*) And the prices he pays makes the silver look like peanuts! (*Crosses, sits* R. C. *chair.*) They hooked you, Daddy, I told him—the silver was the come-on—and now they've got you by the well-known chandeliers. He gave me a picture for Christmas that year, and I yelled bloody murder. Two months later I watched him sell it for a twenty-thousand dollar profit—a picture of two apples and a piece of grapefruit rind, it looked to me like. (*Rises, crosses* U. C.) Do you see what I mean, Stella?

STELLA. I begin to.

FRANCES. It was the same all the way down the line. Every jerk thing he did. The house in the country—ninety-seven rooms—I think there's still a St. Bernard dog lost up on the third floor—turns out to be a wonderful buy. (*Crosses to* R. C. *chair.*) And the wine cellar, and the stuff I thought was broken-down kitchen furniture, and he's (*Crosses above* R. C. *chair.*) *really* gone nuts, is genuine French Provincial. (*Crosses above sofa.*) So when he tells me about this wonderful play and how he's going to stick a Roman candle into the tired face of show business, I decided to give a little shove myself. One shove for a hundred and fifty thousand dollars, (*Crosses and sits sofa.*) that's what *I* got, Stella. Now you tell *me* something.

STELLA. What?

FRANCES. What the hell is that play about?

STELLA. It's an allegory.

FRANCES. What's that?

STELLA. (*Shrugs.*) That's what the man in the back of me said and he looked like he knew what he was talking about. In the middle of the first act he said, " This play is either an allegory or the biggest joke ever played on the City of Boston."

FRANCES. Some joke.

STELLA. A little while later he said, " By God—they're *not* joking —it *is* an allegory! " And he left.

FRANCES. Well, that's a help. At least I can tell my friends I dropped a hundred and fifty thousand bucks in an allegory— maybe they'll think it's some kind of an oil well.

STELLA. (*R., crossing* C.) Oh, what difference does it make, Frances! Suppose you *did* know what it was? You don't have to know what an egg is to open it and smell it, do you? (*The Shriners are heard outside the door yelling, singing and blowing horns.*) That's all we need, (*Rises, crosses* U. *to bar, puts down glass.*) up here with an allegory, and the Shriners are in town.— I'll tell you what I don't understand, Frances.

FRANCES. What?

STELLA. (*Crossing to* R. C. *chair.*) Irene. I know my daughter like a book, and believe me, she's crazy like a fox. She never does anything without knowing exactly what the percentage is, backwards and forwards. (*Crosses to* L. C. *chair.*) She must have had some reason for doing this. (*Crosses* L. C.)

FRANCES. Maybe she wanted to get even with somebody. Did Sidney ever louse her up in some way?

STELLA. (*Impatiently.*) Oh, no. Besides, if you want to get even with a producer you talk him into doing an Ibsen revival. (*Crosses above drum table.*)

FRANCES. She thought it was good, that's all. Like Sidney. This time he *really* bought two apples and a piece of grapefruit rind. And your friend Carleton is the grapefruit rind, if you ask me.

I could cry, he says. He should drop dead! I wouldn't let him put on a girdle for me—much less a play!

STELLA. (*Crossing to R. C. chair.*) I don't know about him, and I don't know about Sidney, either, but I do know about Irene, and I tell you this doesn't make sense. It just doesn't! (*Crosses C.*) Or just about as much sense as her marrying Tyler did. Couldn't figure that one out, either.

FRANCES. What's her marrying Tyler got to do with all this?

STELLA. Did you ever get a full load of my son-in-law, Frances?

FRANCES. No. He never opens his mouth around me.

STELLA. He will. Once or twice a year he opens his mouth—like when the slush melts—and I go and visit my sister in Florida. (*Crosses above drum table.*)

FRANCES. But he's something big in Wall Street, (STELLA *turns.*) isn't he? I thought that was why she married him.

STELLA. Listen—(*Crossing to sofa.*) Irene didn't have to marry Wall Street money, dear—we've socked away plenty. (*Sits.*) I saw to that. Why, before she was old enough to *read* she knew how to order two breakfasts from Room Service and only pay for one. She didn't marry Tyler for money, Frances.

FRANCES. Don't tell me it was love!

STELLA. No—not unless you can imagine someone falling in love with a tree.

FRANCES. All right. What the hell was it?

STELLA. It was just what she wanted—she had it all figured out—and I was too dumb to catch on. This time she married for comfort—and it worked out fine. Why, the funny thing is now even *I'm* fond of Tyler. Besides, not many husbands would stand for me, and naturally I go with the lease. Of course, there are times when he does certain things that I have to stop and say to myself: "What would I do if I were a horse?" But then I do—and I kind of see his viewpoint. (*Door opens and* TYLER RAYBURN *comes into the room, puts coat on door chair, looking very fine indeed in his dinner clothes.*) Why, hello, Tyler.

TYLER. (*Crossing D. C.*) Hello, Mother. Went extremely well tonight, didn't it?

FRANCES. Huh?

TYLER. I said it went extremely well.

FRANCES. What theater were *you* at?

TYLER. I went to see "Oklahoma." Irene said she didn't want me to come until tomorrow night.

FRANCES. Oh. Well, at the theater we were at we could have used " Oklahoma." We could have used lantern slides.

TYLER. You mean it didn't go very well, Mother?

STELLA. No, it did not go very well, Tyler. No use keeping secrets from you. You'd catch on by tomorrow night when you found yourself all alone in that big theater.

TYLER. (*Laughing*.) Now, now, it never goes well that first time, does it? You know that, Mother.

STELLA. It never went like this, dear. And I've seen 'em go all different ways in my time. This was a brand new way, Tyler.

TYLER. (*Laughing*.) You're always too critical, you people. Now, me—I'm just John Q. Public. (*Crosses to bar, gets drink.*)

STELLA. Oh, that's who you are, dear.

TYLER. You know what I mean, Mother.

STELLA. Yes, (*Rises.*) I know what you mean, dear. You see how I have to keep asking myself that question? (STELLA *crosses* L. C. *chair—sits.*)

TYLER. (*Crossing* D. R. C.) Where is everybody, by the way?

FRANCES. Hiding, I guess.

TYLER. Oh, come, come—aren't you being a trifle precipitate, Mrs. Black?

FRANCES. (*Laughing*.) Just a trifle. But stick around, Bud—I'm gonna be a good deal more of whatever that is when *Mr*. Black gets here. I'm gonna be real snazzy with Mr. Black.

TYLER. (*Laughing*.) You artists! Now, just suppose we behaved this way down in Wall Street every time a stock didn't do well, h'm? Why, there wouldn't be a stock-broker left!

FRANCES. That's bad, huh?

TYLER. I mean, you see, that *we* have our dreams and our disappointments, too. I often say it's very much like the theater. Same thing! For instance, you float an issue of Canandaigue Copper, you manipulate it on the Board three ways from Sunday, and the public won't buy a share of it. Finally, you split it (*Crosses above sofa* C.) two for one. Just like the theater, isn't it? What?

FRANCES. I didn't say a damn thing, Mr. Rayburn.

TYLER. Well, there you have it. Same thing! (*Crosses* U. R. C.) Mother, did you order the cold cuts and chicken à la king from Room Service? Irene asked me to remind you.

STELLA. No, I didn't, Tyler. Anyone around this show who wants to eat on his own. I wouldn't give 'em one of J. J.'s polly-seeds. (TYLER *crosses* U. R. *Door opens and* SIDNEY *comes in. His hat is*

31

pulled low over his eyes, his coat collar is turned up, and his hands pushed deep in his pockets. He kicks door shut behind him, grunts, and puts coat, hat, and scarf on door chair, and walks to window where he stands looking out, his back to the others. Finally:)

FRANCES. (*Sweetly.*) Well, you sure stuck a Roman candle in the tired face of show business, Daddy. (*Silence.*)

STELLA. I think he stuck it some place else, and it went off, too. (SIDNEY *flings around. He is in a terrible mood. He glares at them both as if he might devastate them with a word—then crosses to phone and picks it up.*)

SIDNEY. Let me talk to Miss Morrison, please—chief night operator. Excuse me if I find out what some plain citizens think— instead of listening to Shubert Alley wiseacres. (*Into phone.*) Hello—Miss Morrison? Sidney Black. I left two complimentary tickets at the box office for you. How did you like the show? You couldn't go? Well, did you send anybody? Your mother and father? How did they like it? Have you heard from them? They want to know what is it? (*Hangs up phone.*) PEASANTS! (*Crosses* U. C.)

FRANCES. Does that wind up the plain citizens, Daddy? Would you like to hear what a plain wife thought?

SIDNEY. (*Crossing* R. C.) I knew what you thought. I know just the way you think. That's why you're still on skates.

FRANCES. (*Rising and going around sofa to* SIDNEY.) Okay, lover, so you want to fight, huh? Well, put 'em up!

TYLER. (*Crossing* D. *between* SIDNEY *and* FRANCES.) Now, now, Mrs. Black—Mr. Black! We can't always produce " Oklahoma," can we?

SIDNEY. What the hell has (*Crossing* U. L.) " Oklahoma " got to do with this?

FRANCES. How (*Crossing* D. *to* C.) do you like that, Stella! He's sore! On my money!

SIDNEY. Oh! (*Crosses* D. *to* FRANCES.) So Mrs. Big Mouth held a press conference, eh? Well, you cried to get in, so don't come crying around now. And stop needling me, Frances. I got work to do. I don't intend to take this lying down. (FRANCES *turns her back.*)

STELLA. Standing up *is* better. You can see where the stuff that's hitting you is coming from.

SIDNEY. (*Whirling on her.*) Listen, (*Crosses to* STELLA.) my

32

friend—I'd advise you to stay out of this. Well out. I'm in no mood for the underground. (*Crosses* U. L. *A knock at door.* FRANCES *sits arm of* R. C. *chair.*)

STELLA. Come in. That good luck telegram from Reubens always arrives about now. (*But it is* CARLETON *who enters. He stands for a moment in doorway—a simple martyr—a bit of the true cross.*) Come in! Oh, hello, dear. (*To* CARLETON.) We were wondering where you were. (*Front.*) I thought maybe you and that little old scrubwoman were tearing a mop together. (SIDNEY *crosses* U. *to windows.*)

CARLETON. (*At* U. C.) How amusing you are, Stella. How amusing it always is to see a noble work misunderstood.

FRANCES. Yeah, I could cry.

CARLETON. As a matter of fact, I have been sitting alone in my room for the last half hour in the dark—(*Crosses* U. *to bar.*) I have been thinking. Thinking about the Greeks during their great period.

FRANCES. Smart, oh, very smart. Just the thing to do at a time like this, wouldn't you say, Stella? (*Rises.*) My money's on him. (*Sits* R. C. *chair.*) Oiy, is my money on him!

CARLETON. (*Crossing* D. C.) That dreadful, stupid audience! This play escaped them completely. This play is completely Greek.

FRANCES. Shake, brother.

CARLETON. It's in the great tradition of Greek drama, and Greek drama in its origin was a ritual performed for a religious purpose. Its object was not to entertain the spectators.

STELLA. Well, we were right back there with the Greeks tonight, weren't we?

CARLETON. Actually the word drama is a transliteration of the Greek opaua, which means a thing done, while Theater is a transliteration of the Greek theatron, which means a seeing place. Even the word audience, meaning those who listen, is derived from the Latin and therefore represents a later idea of playgoing. It is from the use of two Greek words and one Latin word that a most useful hint is given us as to the very first dramatic values.

FRANCES. Thank you, Blossom Seeley. (*Rises, crosses to* D. R.)

TYLER. (*Singing softly.*) " I'm just a girl who can't say no— (CARLETON *crosses* U. R. C., SIDNEY *crosses* D. *above drum table*) de-de-de-de-de-de. I'm justa . . ." (*They all turn and stare at him, he stops.*) I beg your pardon!

CARLETON. (*Crossing* U. C.) Forgive my asking, (*Crosses and sits sofa.*) Stella, but is there going to be any food? I'm famished. (SIDNEY *crosses* U. *to bar.*)

STELLA. No, Carleton, there is not going to be any food. In fact, from now on, I wish you'd all use your own matches. (*Door bursts open and* IRENE *stands resplendent in doorway—shimmering low-cut evening dress, sables thrown lightly across her shoulders, diamonds glittering from her ears, her neck and her fingers. In one hand, incongruously enough, she holds some string from which six colored balloons float.*)

IRENE. (*At* U. C., *coming in as* STELLA *rises and crosses* D. L.) Darlings, aren't they fun? Peter bought them for me, on the way in tonight. There was a man selling them just at the stage entrance, and I said, " Peter—look—balloons! That's great good luck, you know." And he bought them for me. Tyler, hold them for a moment. (*Crosses to him.*)

TYLER. Where do you want them, dear?

IRENE. Oh, darling, after six years of marriage I shouldn't think I'd have to tell you where I want something after (*Above* R. C. *chair.*) an exhausting opening night.

TYLER. Well, Irene, I wouldn't like to just put them in the bedroom, because ——

SIDNEY. Excuse me. (IRENE *turns, puts cape on door chair.*) Forgive me, Irene, but would you like a *report* on how the play went, or would you rather concentrate on the balloons? We have many problems to face—but I had no idea we had a balloon problem, but by all means let us solve it. Where do you want the balloons?

IRENE. Darling, (*Crossing above* R. C. *chair.*) I don't care where they're put—it just looks silly to see Tyler standing there holding them. All right, Sidney, what was wrong?

SIDNEY. Number one —— (*A knock at door.*)

IRENE. Come in! (PETER *comes into room. He looks haggard and drawn and avoids meeting anyone's eyes. Crosses* D. *to* R. C. *chair.*)

SIDNEY. Where the hell have you been? Where the hell have you been since the end of the second act?

PETER. Walking. Sorry. (*Above* R. C. *chair.*)

SIDNEY. Well, sit down. And prepare to give out with a two-syllable word once in a while. We're in trouble. Three hundred thousand dollars' worth of trouble. (*Crosses* C.)

FRANCES. Some fine way to talk to the Salzburg Festival!

SIDNEY. (*Crossing above sofa—warningly.* PETER *sits* R. C. *chair.*) Do me a favor, Frances—get lost, will ya!

34

FRANCES. (*Rising.*) Deal 'em up, Stella. Daddy's going to shake hands with Tchaikowsky's Fifth again! (*She goes toward card table, sits* L. C. *chair.*)

SIDNEY. (*Crossing above drum table.*) You two are not going to sit down and start playing that cockamamie game *now!*

STELLA. Just until the lifeboats are lowered, dear. (*She joins* FRANCES *at table.*)

SIDNEY. (*Crossing above drum table.*) Well, I'll be goddamned if I'm going to stand around and watch *gin* being played while ——

IRENE. (*Crossing* D. *to* C.) Just a moment, Sidney! I will not have that sort of language used in front of my mother.

SIDNEY. (*Crossing to* IRENE *at* C.) Your mother? You mean Stella?

IRENE. (*Crossing to* STELLA—*above* L. *chair.*) I've had all sorts of managers in my time, darling, and I've never allowed them to say an ugly word in the presence of my mother.

SIDNEY. I guess she must have picked it up from the kids in the street.

IRENE. (*Crossing* C.) And while we're on the subject of managers, darling, may I tell you that in all my years in the theater, you are the first one who lacked the taste or the manners to come backstage and thank me for my performance. Good or bad! (*Crosses above drum table.*)

SIDNEY. (*Crossing* C.) You mean a manager is supposed to come back and thank you for a bad performance? (*Crosses above sofa.*) All right. Thank you.

IRENE. *What* did you say then, darling?

SIDNEY. You hear well enough when *terms* are discussed, old head-in-the-clouds!

PETER. (*As* SIDNEY *crosses* D. R.) Look—whatever blame there is, is mine. Couldn't we just skip all this and ——

IRENE. (*Crossing* C.) Tyler, did you hear that? Mother, you heard it, of course? Our little friend is judging acting now. My dears, not figure eights—*acting!* (*Crosses above sofa to* CARLETON.) Darling, don't open your mouth and show everybody what rink you come from!

SIDNEY. (*Crossing below sofa to* IRENE C.) I'll tell you what kind of a rink I come from, Miss Livingston! I've got three hundred thousand dollars sunk in this jamboree, but that wouldn't stop me from closing it tonight. Not tomorrow night.

IRENE. (*Crossing above* SIDNEY *to* TYLER, *bringing him* C. SIDNEY *crosses above drum table to* D. L.) Tyler, darling, did you hear

35

what the little man said? We're closing tonight! Do you know what that means, dear? You can take me duck-shooting with you this year, darling, just as we've always planned.

TYLER. That's smashing, Irene ——

IRENE. We'll lie in the blinds together, Tyler, and laugh at all the silly people getting ready to play matinees. Break a balloon with me, darling, we're closing. (*She pops a balloon.*) Bang! Got him, Tyler. (*She pops another.*) Bang! There's a brace of them.

STELLA. (CARLETON *rises and crosses* U. *in alcove, sits on piano stool.*) Bang! That's gin, Frances.

SIDNEY. Shut up, shut up, *SHUT UP!* All of you! (*All turn and look.*) Now, listen to me! And not a word out of any of you! (TYLER *crosses* U. *in alcove,* IRENE *crosses* U. *to bar. Strangely enough, there is silence. His face is so violent that they all stare at him fascinated.*) We're going to stop talking about everything else and we're going to talk about this play! Nothing but this play! (*Crosses below across stage to* D. R.) I'll hear from you one at a time, and anyone who interrupts can pick up his teeth outside. All right. You're first, Peter. You wrote it. Got anything to say?

PETER. (*Rising and crossing* R., *across sofa.*) I believe in this play. And I'll work like hell to fix it. All I need to know is that *you* still do.

SIDNEY. Never mind whether we believe in it—we're stuck with it, bub! (*Crosses above sofa to* C.) And I don't intend to be stuck with it, ladies and gentlemen! Not for a minute. Before that wise mob gives *me* the horse laugh, I'll laugh it up *for* 'em! (PETER *sits sofa.*) I'll put a line of girls in it and Olsen and Johnson, if necessary. So let's quit horsing around with what we believe in and get down to cases. Okay, Irene, you got anything to say?

IRENE. Plenty! (*Crossing to* SIDNEY U. C.) But to start with, is there any earthly reason, in that first scene, why I should not be wearing a smart afternoon dress instead of those rags Mr. Fitzgerald has me walking around in? Second, is there any reason why ——

CARLETON. (*Crossing to above phone table.*) I am not interrupting —I am merely pointing out that the first scene of this play is the ruins of Radio City, and the bomb has fallen just one hour before.

IRENE. What of it? She might have just been coming out of The Stork Club and been caught in the crowd. (SIDNEY *crosses above sofa, to piano, sits piano stool.*) All they saw tonight was a great

36

mob of extras groaning and dying. It was twenty minutes before they knew I was on the stage at all. (*Crosses* L.)

CARLETON. (*Above* R. C. *chair.*) What do you want to do, dear? Rush on in a smart afternoon dress to the ruins of Radio City and say: "Is anything the matter?" Talk sense, my dear. (*Sits* R. C. *chair.*)

IRENE. Sense—sense!

PETER. Wait, please, everybody! I know you're disappointed and upset ——

IRENE. Just a trifle upset! (*Crosses* U. L.)

PETER. All of this is my fault ——

CARLETON. Really? I thought it was all my fault!

PETER. After all, this is my first play.

IRENE. We know, dear.

PETER. I had to learn what you can give an audience and what you can't.

CARLETON. We did, too.

PETER. Look—I'm trying. Let me speak. (*Rises, crosses to* R. *end of sofa.*) There are things I can do that will help this play. When they laughed they were right. I was being pompous and they saw through me. I can say the same things and make it simpler and more honest. I know I can.

SIDNEY. (*Rises, crosses* D. *above sofa.*) Look, Jack. Simplicity and honesty we got plenty of in this play. What we need are a few laughs and a little schmaltz.

PETER. Laughs?

SIDNEY. Yes, laughs. What's the matter with laughs? To hell with telling 'em anything—let's give 'em a show.

PETER. Look—all this play has got—the thing that made you do it —work the way you all did, is what it had to say. If you try to make it into something else, we'll be left with nothing!

IRENE. As against what we've got now, of course!

PETER. That's all we've got—believe me! That's what made you want to do the play! That's what made me want to write it. Good or bad, don't run out on that now, or we haven't got a chance.

SIDNEY. (*Quietly.*) The only chance we've got, my friend, is to forget what made us do this play—God alone knows what made you write it—so let's put the cover over the ashcan and when we need any more two-for-a-quarter beauty and poetry—you'll be right here and we'll turn around and ask you for some. (*Crosses* C.) Meanwhile, I don't want to hear any private battles between you two about extras and clothes. If you don't want to talk turkey—— (*But the* PARROT *breaks in.*) Shut up and I'll do the talking. And I'm going to talk fast, too!

PARROT. Bless you, darling! Bang! Bless you, darling! Bang! (IRENE *crosses* U. *in alcove to piano.*) Bless you, darling! Bang!

SIDNEY. (*Thin-lipped.*) Get that talking vulture out of here!

STELLA. (*Rising, crossing* C. *to* SIDNEY.) Are you by any chance referring to J. J., dear?

SIDNEY. I'll change it. I'm referring to *both* talking vultures, (PETER *crosses* D., *sits sofa.*) you *and* that bird. I'd like you *both* out of here. In fact, I'd like nobody here but the star, the author and the director of this sterling silver schmageggie. That includes you, Mrs. Bigbrain, my wife, and John Q. Public. And if you have any suggestions on how to fix this play—send the parrot up with them. (*Crosses below to* D. R.) Meanwhile—scatter!

IRENE. (*So sweetly, crossing* D. *to* C.) Tyler, dear, would you fetch that nice mystery book you brought up with you?—We're going to bed. No need for anyone to scatter—whatever that communist expression means. We're going to bed.

SIDNEY. Oh, no, you're not going to bed!

IRENE. Be careful, darling! Oh, do be careful. You've insulted my husband, my dear mother, and made cruel remarks about an innocent bird that has been a family pet for years.

STELLA. (*Crossing* D. *above sofa.*) A bird, by the way, that has sat in on more hits than you'll ever see, Mr. Black.

IRENE. Oh, shut up, Mother!

STELLA. Don't tell me to shut up, Irene. (SIDNEY *sits desk chair* D. R.)

TYLER. (*Crossing* L. *above sofa.*) My dear, I can't seem to *find* that book.

IRENE. Well, come to bed, anyway—that'll be mystery enough. (*Crosses above* R. C. *chair.*) And here, darling—(*Crosses* D. *to* CARLETON—*puts necklace around his neck.*) here is Duse's necklace! Hang it around a neck more worthy than mine. Hang it around your wife's neck, dear. If it doesn't fit, I know a number of people who will be glad to tighten it. (*Crosses* U. R.)

CARLETON. (*Livid. Rising.*) Miss Livingston either makes a public apology to my wife, Mr. Black, or I do not appear at another rehearsal. Lawyers hitched to horses couldn't drag me to a rehearsal of this show now, until that woman apologizes for insulting one of our leading actresses.

STELLA. (*Crossing* L. C.) Leading actress, who counted the votes, dear—you? (*Crosses* L.)

CARLETON. That's *two* apologies I want now, Mr. Black. (*Sits chair* R. C.)

IRENE. (*Crossing to* STELLA *at* C.) Mother, will you kindly shut up!

STELLA. (*Crossing to* IRENE.) Don't keep telling me to shut up, Irene! That trust fund's in my name—so watch your language! (*Crosses above* L. *chair*.)

IRENE. (*Crossing* U. *in alcove to piano. Emotionally*.) Take me away, Tyler, oh, Tyler, take me away and give me a child—a child that won't turn on me—at least until it's older. Let me have a few good years—I need them—I deserve them—all my life I've worked and slaved—and for what? For this! To have everyone torture me—to have my own mother turn on me. Oh, Tyler—it's too much—it's the last straw. Let us have children—I know when I'm beaten! (*She exits up* R., *slams door*.)

STELLA. (*Crossing* C.) The spirits of ammonia are in the medicine chest, (TYLER *crosses* U., *exits in alcove bedroom*.) the hot water bag is in the closet and you can get ice from Room Service for the cold compresses, Tyler. Anybody else want to tell me to shut up?

TYLER. (*Entering and crossing* D. *two steps*.) Some day, Mother, I'm going to put my foot down! Some day I'm going to forget I'm a Harvard man—Mother. (*He exits, slamming door*.)

FRANCES. (*Rising and crossing above sofa to* R. *end*.) Okay, Pops, on your feet, this was just the warm-up—the prelims—you ain't even smelled the canvas yet, lover. Mrs. Bigbrain, eh? That's why I'm still on skates, huh? Come on, Daddy, get 'em up! Let's see your footwork in the main event.

SIDNEY. (*Rising and crossing below to bar*.) I'll talk to you later, Frances. I've got a lot on my mind right now.

FRANCES. Well, you better have me on your mind, lamb-pie, or your wife closes in Boston, too . . .

CARLETON. (*Rising*.) Excuse me. I have something to say to Mr. Black.

FRANCES. Make it fast, will you, bub—I've been trying to get on here myself for half an hour!

CARLETON. (*Crossing* U. *to door* C.) Since I have no intention of ever speaking again to anyone connected with this play for the rest of my life, I shall say what I intend to say. Mr. Black, I think —you stink! (*He exits* C., SIDNEY *takes drink*.)

FRANCES. (*Taking furs from desk chair and crossing above sofa to* U. C.) Isn't he cute, Daddy, he thinks you only stink.

SIDNEY. I'm warning you, Frances. Don't tangle with me. I'm going to take a walk, I may walk all night. Give me the key to the room.

FRANCES. (*Coat up, crosses above sofa to door.*) Just knock! I'll have all the furniture moved to one side. So come out of your corner fighting. Don't throw away these flowers, Stella, or the balloons, I may open a stand in Shubert Alley, and I'll need some merchandise—flowers, balloons, my husband just produced an allegory—(*Crosses* U. *to door.*) poor old Broadway Frances, flowers, balloons. (*She exits* C.)

SIDNEY. (*Crossing to chair, gets coat, crosses to above sofa.*) When I decide what to do with this three hundred thousand dollars' worth of sheep dip . . . I'll let you know.—Daahhh. (*He exits* C.)

STELLA. (*Crossing* U. *to door.*) When *he* decides! Huh! (*Crosses* D. C.) If I know my daughter, Mr. Sloan, she's getting laryngitis right now. Stick around, Mr. Sloan, and you'll hear coughing start coming from that bedroom in a few minutes, that'll make Camille sound like she had nothing but hay fever. (*Crosses above sofa.*) Don't go blaming yourself, Mr. Sloan. It's not your fault. All kinds of nuts write plays—but no one's fool enough to do 'em. I don't blame you for this one bit. (*Phone rings. She picks up receiver.*) Hello? Who? Peter? Oh, yes—yes. Just a minute. It's for you—a lady. It's all right—take it right here. Just going to put the cover over J. J. (*Closes cover.*) and (*Crosses* D. *to* D. L. *door, taking whisky bottle.*) I'm going to bed with my opening night ovaltine. (*Exits.* PETER *walks to phone and for a moment hesitates. Then picks it up resolutely.*)

PETER. (*Into phone.*) Helen? Hello, darling! I couldn't call you— I've been up here in Miss Livingston's room. (*A pause. Then:*) Brace yourself, baby. It's a bust—a complete and absolute failure. Now, take it easy—you've got to believe it—it's true. No—not *any* of it. I didn't even see the third act—they started to laugh and I couldn't stand it. (*He listens for a moment.*) No, Helen— please, don't! Please! I don't want you to come up—I don't want you to see it! It's just—too painful, that's why. I didn't know what it was like—it's awful, Helen. A kind of naked, personal exposure. Oh, to hell with it! So I can't write! Maybe it's better to get it this way and stop fooling yourself. I'll talk to you tomorrow—it won't seem so bad tomorrow—I just can't talk about it now. Sure, I'll call every day—it helps. It's helped right now. Baby, sure it would help to have you here—but I don't want you to come up—I kinda have to go through this part of it alone. Okay. I promise. As soon as I open my eyes in the morning. Good night, darling. (*A slow smile comes over his face as he listens.*) Good night, baby. (*Crosses* D. *to* R. C. *chair. Sits. Shriner—*MAX*—enters* C. *door.*)

MAX. Is this (*Crosses* D. *to* C., *to* PETER.) Jim Unger's room, buddy?

SHRINER. Do you know where Jim Unger's room is, buddy?

OTHER SHRINERS. (*Off-stage.*) Hey, Max, come on—you're holding up the parade.

MAX. (U. *to door.*) Keep your pants on, I'm coming! If you see Jim Unger (*Crosses* D. C.)—you can't miss him—he's an ugly little runt with a big fat behind and a cigar in his mouth . . . tell him Max (*Crosses* U. *to door.*) is down in the bar ripping up the joint. (*Wolf calls and whistles off-stage.* OWEN *and* MISS LOWELL *appear.* MAX, *to* MISS LOWELL.) Why, hello, honey. If you can shake the stiff you're with, I'll be down in the bar. (MISS LOWELL *sweeps past him, puts fur on window chair and sits* L. *chair.*) No offense, Jack. (*He goes.* OWEN *shuts door, crosses* D. *above* L. C. *chair.*)

OWEN. It's always so helpful to open a show with a convention in town. I missed you at the theater, Mr. Sloan.

PETER. (*Rising and crossing above* R. C. *chair.*) I wasn't there after the second act.

OWEN. I know what you must have been going through.

PETER. (*Crossing* U. *in alcove.*) No, you don't. You can't imagine.

OWEN. Yes, I can. I've had my nights in the back of a theater. Your play is a lot better than it looked tonight, Mr. Sloan. A lot of it was very touching and very true.

PETER. They laughed. They walked out on it.

MISS LOWELL. I didn't. I was very moved.

OWEN. It's the work you do on the play from now on, Peter, that's going to make all the difference between success and failure.

PETER. Is it? Well, I'm *not* going to do any work on this play, Mr. Turner.

OWEN. Why not?

PETER. (*Crossing* D. *above sofa.*) You weren't up here just now—you don't know what happened up here. You don't know what they were like! (*Crosses above sofa to* D. R.)

41

OWEN. Oh, I'm sure they behaved badly . . . they're all old friends. But why should it surprise you so, Peter, that this, too, should be a part of it?

PETER. Why? Oh, it surprises the hell out of me, Mr. Turner. Because I know now that a lot of things I thought were true— things I believed in pretty deeply or I couldn't have written that play at all—are just plain childish!

OWEN. Not to me they weren't. It was wonderful to hear that kind of talk in the theater again.

PETER. Was it? Well, I'm embarrassed now by all that wide-eyed idealism. I couldn't go back (*Crosses below sofa to* C.) and work on that play—I'd die laughing.

OWEN. (*Grabbing* PETER'S *arm, stops him* C.) Now wait a minute, Peter. You're too close to something really good.

PETER. Look, Mr. Turner—it's damn nice of you to do this—to care about what happens to me or my play. I'm not ungrateful, believe me. But I'm walking out on more than just this play. I'm walking out on a lot of my own half-baked ideas that make me want to laugh now—just the way that audience did. Sidney Black and company have shown me just what the score is. (*Crosses* U. *to bar—back to audience, takes drink.*)

OWEN. (*Sitting* R. C. *chair.*) My first play opened in this town, Peter. Twenty-two years ago . . . and I think if somebody had said to me, choose between having this play a success and losing your right arm, I'd have cheerfully given up my right arm. Well, it wasn't a success—and afterwards, right in this hotel, I went through just what you did tonight. May have been this very room, for all I know. I had my own Sidney, Irene and Carleton. And I felt just the way you do now. But I stayed. It wasn't easy—but I stayed. Why? Because I thought I had something to say and I wasn't going to let anything or anybody stop me from saying it. (*Rises, crosses* U. *to* PETER.) And if you walk out of that door now, Peter, there's a very good chance that you may never write another line. I mean that. A young writer like yourself sometimes stands right on the brink—it can go either way—a wrong push and he never comes back!

PETER. (*Crossing* U. *to windows.*) I was kicked over the edge half an hour ago, Mr. Turner. I don't want to come back. (*Crosses to below sofa.*) I was willing to work my head off—why, I've got ten times more at stake than they have! I've got a girl—we want to get married—we've been waiting two years for this—I just

42

heard her trying not to cry on the phone—because she knows what this means for both of us. This isn't easy for me to walk out of. But I'm going to—because the only thing I've got left now is knowing what the score is—at least I learned *that* (*Crosses to desk.*) tonight—and boy, I'm going to hang on to it. (*Crosses above sofa.*) So don't fall for that fine talk you heard on the stage tonight, Mr. Turner! I wrote it, and I tell you it's a fake! The thunder is fake—the stage hands make it—and those fine, brave, big words are as hollow as the people who spoke them! (*Picks up phone.*) Hello, operator, get me the airport, will you?

MISS LOWELL. Well, there goes the ball game.

OWEN. Yep! (*Crosses above drum table.*)

PETER. Hello, airport? What's the next plane out? To New York? No, I can't make that, I've got to pack. What's the next? Four-thirty? Fine. One seat, Peter Sloan. Right. American Airlines? Thanks. I'll pick it up at the window. Thanks, Mr. Turner. (*Crosses* R. C.) Thank you. Very much. And I hope you can forgive what must seem like my silliness and downright stubbornness. I don't expect you to understand it—I only know that for me it's right. Anyway, thanks. I'll leave a note for Sidney—no use writing three notes all saying the same thing. Is there anything else I ought to do, Mr. Turner?

OWEN. (*Crossing* L. C.) No. Unless you want to make one final bow to an old tradition of the Dramatists' Guild.

PETER. What's that?

OWEN. Griddle cakes at Childs'. Always at about three o'clock on the night of an out-of-town opening, we find ourselves at Childs' having griddle cakes. Don't ask me why. Perhaps it's a playwright's splendid gesture of defiance at the audience, the critics, and the general hell that's coming. Because those griddle cakes stay right here—(*He points to his chest.*) for about three days, and you know it with every bite. Can you pack quickly? We'll drive you out to the airport from Childs'. (*Crosses above* L. C. *chair.*) You're included, Miss Lowell—you're practically an honorary member, after tonight. (MISS LOWELL *rises, gets furs. As they go toward door.*) By the way—I'd like to deliver that note to Sidney for you myself. That all right with you?

PETER. Sure.

MISS LOWELL. (*Crossing* U. *to door.*) I want to be right here when you do it, Mr. Turner. May I?

OWEN. (*As* MISS LOWELL *exits, leaving door open.*) Certainly.—

Yes, sir, I'll deliver that note personally. (*Crosses to* PETER.) What a malicious old bastard I am!—but oh, how I've earned it through the years. Come on, (*Crosses* U. *to door.*) I've started to butter those griddle cakes. (*Exits.* PETER *stands in door, looks around room, makes gesture of finality—exits. For a long moment room remains in darkness and no sound is heard. Then: from* IRENE'S *room,* TYLER *comes out, stumbles at piano bench. He knocks on* STELLA'S *door as he is* D. L.)

TYLER. Mother? (*Crosses above sofa.*) You'd better come out! You'd better come out right away!

STELLA. (*Entering in negligee.*) What is it, Tyler? (*Crosses* C.) I was just going to bed. (*Suddenly, the shrill blast of a trumpet is heard outside in the hall and a group of drunken male voices singing " Margie " to the trumpet's blare. Then comes a woman's scream of terror, and some drunken laughter.*)

TYLER. Irene's losing her voice, Mother. It's going faster than it's ever gone before!

STELLA. All right, dear. You go back to bed, and I'll call Dr. Schollus. (*Crosses to phone. Noise of Shriners outside.*) Oh, those goons! (*Crosses out in* C. *hall. She goes to door and stands in hall.*) Go on—get out of here! Get away from this door—go be funny some place else.

A SHRINER. Hello, Peachy! Cookie, do you do the samba?

TYLER. Stand aside, (*Crosses out in hall.*) Mother!—I'll handle these ruffians. (*He goes past her.*) Now, look here, you fellows ——

A SHRINER. Oh! A spoilsport! (*Punch!* TYLER *staggers back holding his eye—*STELLA *helping him.*)

IRENE. (*Staggering out of her room, and crossing* D. *above sofa.*) All this noise! What *is* all this racket!

TYLER. I got hit! A Shriner hit me!

IRENE. (*Crossing* D. C.) I do think, Tyler, that with your wife very ill, you might do me the courtesy of not indulging in vicious street brawls. (TYLER *crosses* U. *in alcove.*)

SIDNEY. (*Crossing* D. L. C. *Enters as* IRENE *sits* R. C. *chair.*) I just took a walk. It's a cold night and I came to a cold decision. The show is opening in New York as per schedule. I'm in so deep, a few thousand more won't make any difference. All I want now out of this whole thing is to read those notices the next morning on you and Carleton Fitzgerald. (IRENE *coughs.*) You're coming in clear as a bell, but you're under contract to me and you're going to open.

IRENE. You'll never get me to New York in this show. You're lucky if I play tomorrow night.

TYLER. Careful, Irene, you'll lose your voice.

IRENE. That's what I'm trying to do, you fool! (*Rises.*) Oh, my God, I'm married to Mortimer Snerd. Pneumonia! (*Crosses to* SIDNEY.) That's what I want, pneumonia. The peace and quiet of an oxygen tent where I can't hear any of you.

SIDNEY. You'll play this show, Miss Livingston, if you have to do it with your head sticking out of an iron lung! (IRENE *sits* R. C. *chair.* IRENE *coughs.*) Three of my nephews are doctors, and they'll be there at every performance.

CURTAIN

ACT III

The same. Stage is in darkness and silence for a few moments. The quiet is shattered by some male voices outside the door.

1ST MAN. Good night, Jack.

2ND MAN. Good night, Ed.

3RD MAN. Good night, Jim. You say you were from Saginaw, Michigan, Jack?

1ST MAN. That's right, Saginaw. Moved to Saginaw from Moline, Illinois, about eleven years ago. You from Elkhart, Indiana?

3RD MAN. That's right, Elkhart. Ever run into a feller called Ben Gitzel in Moline? Hardware supplies. Used to be a feller called Ben Gitzel in Moline about eleven years ago.

1ST MAN. No. There was a Ben Whittaker in Moline 'bout eleven years ago. He was in machine tools. (STELLA *enters from* D. L., *crosses* U. *to* C. *door.*) Can't remember any Ben Gitzel. Well, good night.

2ND MAN. Good night, Jack.

3RD MAN. Good night, Ed.

1ST MAN. Good night, Jim. (STELLA *crosses back toward* D. L., *stops above* L. *chair.*) Say, was Ben Gitzel a short fat feller with a moustache who switched over into plywood?

3RD MAN. That's right. That's Ben Gitzel.

1ST MAN. Why, sure I know Ben Gitzel! What the hell ever happened to him?

3RD MAN. He's got a factory in Elkhart. We sell him all his paper cups.

1ST MAN. You don't say! Little old Ben Gitzel! Little fat feller with a moustache who switched over into plywood? (STELLA *crosses* U. *to* C. *door.*)

3RD MAN. That's right. We sell him all his paper cups. Well, good night, Jack.

2ND MAN. Good night, Ed.

1ST MAN. Good night, Jim. (STELLA *crosses toward* D. L. *door, stops above drum table.*) Say, will you be seeing Ben Gitzel when you get back to Elkhart?

46

3RD MAN. Sure. We sell him all his paper cups. (STELLA *crosses u. to bar, gets empty bottle.*)

1ST MAN. Well, ask Ben Gitzel if he remembers Jack Ebinger, will ya?

3RD MAN. Sure will. Well, good night, Jack.

2ND MAN. Good night, Ed.

1ST MAN. Good night, Jim. (*On third cross, STELLA picks up a bottle from bar and marches determinedly toward door. She opens it to find FRANCES in doorway, hand upraised to knock.*)

FRANCES. (*Crossing D. R. C.*) Hold it, Stella—I'm on your side! (*She closes door.*)

STELLA. They got you up, too, huh? (*Snapping on light, crosses to bar, puts bottle back.*)

FRANCES. (*Crossing to L. C. chair, sits as STELLA crosses above phone table.*) Oh, it's ducky up on our floor! They're tossing fire-crackers into the bathrooms. This is nice and quiet. Better give up on the sleep department, honey, and play some gin with me. The boys are really living tonight!

STELLA. Gin? I won't be able to see the cards, Frances.

FRANCES. Then I got a fighting chance. Come on, Stella—you won't be able to sleep! Let's get some sandwiches and a bottle of beer and make a night of it.

STELLA. (*Picking up phone.*) Make a night of it! I'm getting too old for a lot of Ben Gitzels running around the hall. Hello—give me Room Service. Well, the Shriners are still open! Why don't you shut them up instead of Room Service! (*She bangs up.*) Honest, Frances, (*Crosses D. to below sofa.*) I haven't got the heart to take any more of your money. I'm way ahead right now. I've been running too lucky.

FRANCES. How much are you into me for now, Stella?

STELLA. I don't know—I've got the score inside—but it's plenty. You ought to quit for a while.

FRANCES. (*Rising and crossing to STELLA.*) Want to play a real sporting game? I'll play you a real sporting game, Stella.

STELLA. What?

FRANCES. Three games across—whatever I owe you—against half my interest in the show.

STELLA. Are you kidding, dear?

FRANCES. (*Crossing to L. C. chair, sits.*) No. Let's make it interesting! A real sporting game.

STELLA. (*Crossing C.*) It's interesting, all right. Considering your interest in the show is worth about eleven dollars right now, as I figure it.

FRANCES. (*Rising and crossing* C.) What do you mean? That's a big hunk of show! All that scenery is worth something, isn't it? What about the costumes? All those costumes! I never saw so many people on one stage in my life.

STELLA. Oh, I see what you mean, dear. Salvage!

FRANCES. Sure. It's still worth something, isn't it? The wind machines and the rain effects—and all that scenery. That big staircase, and the mountain with the faces of Washington, Jefferson and Lincoln carved on it! You gotta get *something* back, don't you?

STELLA. (*Crossing to* L. C. *chair.*) This the first show you put money into, Frances?

FRANCES. Yes.

STELLA. (*Sitting* L. C. *chair.*) Well, I'll tell you about the scenery first. You can't sell it—get *that* out of your mind right now—and what's more, you can't even walk away and leave it here.

FRANCES. (*Crossing* D. *around* L. *chair.*) All that scenery?

STELLA. All that scenery! You can't even make believe you forgot about it. No, dear. First you have to pay somebody to have it carted away from the theater—and then you have to pay somebody to burn it.

FRANCES. (*Sitting arm* L. *chair.*) Pay somebody to burn it?

STELLA. Pay somebody to burn it. You and Sidney want to run around the city dump lighting matches? You have to *pay* someone to burn it. Regular union rates, and it's my impression this scenery is going to burn real slow.

FRANCES. Listen, Stella—don't rib me about this. (*Sits* L. *chair.*) My stomach just turned over.

STELLA. I'm just telling you what happens, Frances. You might as well know it.

FRANCES. Yeah. I can tell Sidney. I'll tell him nice and slow—for about two years. Go on, Stella. What happens with the costumes?

STELLA. (*Rising and crossing* C.) Well, in an ordinary show, Frances, a costume that cost two hundred dollars they buy back for about two dollars (*Crosses* L. C. *chair.*) but this is an allegory, dear. The costumes in this show are mostly rags, the survivors of the world are walking around in. Right?

FRANCES. Right! So we get about a dollar apiece for 'em.

STELLA. Oh, no! I wouldn't think so, Frances. What are they going to do with 'em? Can't even cover chairs with 'em!

FRANCES. Can't leave 'em here, either.

STELLA. That's right.

FRANCES. Cart 'em away. Burn 'em. Union rates. Pray for a windy day on the dump so they'll burn fast. Do people who put money into shows know about this, Stella?

STELLA. (*Crossing* R. C. *chair.*) Well, usually a backer gets at least some kind of a souvenir for his dough, Frances. Say, he puts up fifty thousand dollars—he gets a lamp to take home, or his wife gets a pocketbook. (*Crosses* L. C. *chair.*) But you're dealing with an allegory here, Frances. You see anything in this show you can take home?

FRANCES. I got no use for a wind machine. That I know right away.

STELLA. (*Crossing* U. *above drum table.*) You got any place in your house for the mountain with the faces of Washington, Jefferson and Lincoln carved on it? Or the rain effects?

FRANCES. Sidney's bedroom. (STELLA *crosses* R. C.) He should wake up every morning and look at it, and the rain should pour down on him. (*Rises, crosses to* STELLA.) So, actually, Stella, it's going to cost more money, even to close it.

STELLA. Oh, sure. It would be wonderful if you could just stick up a sign saying " gone to lunch " or " if not called for in thirty days, forget it "—but it (*Sits* R. C. *chair.*) just doesn't work that way.

FRANCES. How did you figure my interest was worth eleven dollars, Stella? That's pretty high, isn't it?

STELLA. Well, I wanted to slip it to you easy. This is your first show.

FRANCES. (*Crossing below drum table.*) Yeah. Boy, I can't wait now to run into Irving Berlin. (*Sits edge drum table.*) " There's no business like show business." He ought to be arrested. (*Sits* L. *chair.*) Come on, Stella—deal 'em up. I better start getting some of my dough back.

STELLA. All right, dear. (*Rises, crosses to* L. C. *chair, sits.*) But I'm running too lucky. (*As she starts to deal.*) How'd you and Sidney wind up, Frances? Was it much of a fight?

FRANCES. No, we didn't fight, Stella. You see, I really know what goes on with him. He's quite a guy. It's not the money at all— he just stepped out of his class and he's hurt—and he won't admit

49

it—so he just keeps hollering. (*A knock at door, and before they can say " Come in " the door opens and a* SHRINER *sticks his head in.* STELLA *rises, crosses to bar, picks up bottle.*) On your way, buddy! On your way!

SHRINER. Please, ladies, please! Give me just a moment. I know how you must feel about Shriners!

FRANCES. No, you don't!

SHRINER. Please, ladies. (*Closes door.*) You can see I'm perfectly sober. This *is* Miss Livingston's room, isn't it?

STELLA. What about it?

SHRINER. (STELLA *puts bottle on bar, crosses* D. *above drum table. Crosses* D. C.) I want to apologize to her. I want to apologize to her on behalf of all Shriners—and particularly for those Shriners who were at the theater tonight. I was ashamed of them—ashamed of being a Shriner myself. That beautiful play!

FRANCES. Huh?

SHRINER. Most beautiful play I ever saw—and they damn near ruined it. I got four of them out of the theater myself, and I would have gotten 'em all out, only I didn't want to miss any of it. Most wonderful message in that play, ladies—something for all of us—everybody ought to be made to go and listen to what that play says to all of us.

STELLA. (*Above drum table.*) What does it say?

SHRINER. I don't know. But it was just beautiful—I was all choked up most of the time. (*To* FRANCES.) Excuse me—haven't I seen you on the stage or some place?

FRANCES. You've seen me on skates. Which I don't ever intend to get off again.

SHRINER. Of course! You're Frances Black! Wait till I tell Milly I met Frances Black! (*To* STELLA.) Are you connected with show business, too?

STELLA. I'm connected. Need a new fuse.

SHRINER. (*Crossing* U. *above sofa.*) Well, it sure has been an honor, ladies. To have stood in Irene Livingston's room! Wait till I tell Milly! She's as big a theater (*Crosses* C.) bug as I am! I don't think you folks realize what a boot it is to somebody like my wife or myself to get a (*Crosses to below sofa.*) real smell of the theater.

STELLA. We got plenty of that, all right. Too bad we can't bottle it!

FRANCES. (*Rising and crossing to below* R. C. *chair.*) Wait a minute, Stella. Go ahead, Mr. ——
SHRINER. Gallegher. William H. Gallegher. Excuse me. Just forgot all my manners, I'm so excited. (FRANCES *and* SHRINER *sit,* FRANCES *in* R. C. *chair,* SHRINER *in sofa.*)
FRANCES. You were saying how you loved the theater?
SHRINER. Yessir, I missed the bus somewhere along the line. Always wanted to be in the theater—but my father died while I was still in college, and there I was with four big factories in Elkhart, Indiana. What could I do?
FRANCES. Four factories? You still got 'em?
SHRINER. Five now. Big success—and never did what I really wanted to do! You people are the lucky ones. The theater! What I wouldn't give to be a part of it!
FRANCES. (*Rising and crossing to sofa, sits.*) You know, Mr. Gallegher, you're just saying (STELLA *crosses slowly to above sofa.*) something that strikes close to home. I was saying to my husband, Sidney Black—he produced the show you saw tonight—I was saying to him just this afternoon—Sidney, I said, the trouble with the theater today is that it's a closed corporation. A few big shots run it, and nobody else can get a look-in. You ought to let more people in—real American folks from out of town—like yourself, Mr. Gallegher—those people ought to have a chance to come into the theater. New faces—new blood—new money! I think my husband would be very interested in meeting you, Mr. Gallegher. Let me get him up here. (*Rises and crosses above phone table.*)
SHRINER. Oh, I wouldn't want to trouble him, Mrs. Black. It's very late.
FRANCES. This is no trouble. He'll shoot up here for this. Like a Roman candle.
STELLA. Frances, you make me proud of being a woman!
FRANCES. Operator, get me Mr. Black.
STELLA. Can I give you a drink, Mr. Gallegher? (*Crosses to bar.*) Scotch, Bourbon, Rye, Champagne—anything you want.
SHRINER. No, thanks. I'm drunk enough with just the smell of the theater.
STELLA. (*Crossing above sofa to* R. *arm, sits.*) Chanel Number Five—that's what it is! Chanel Number Five!
FRANCES. Hello? Daddy? I'm with Stella. Can you come up here for a minute, Daddy? I want you to meet somebody. A Mr.

51

Gallegher, from Elkhart, Indiana. (*She makes a face.*) No, Daddy,
I'm not. He's sitting right here and he wants to get into the theater. He wants to get into the theater, Daddy—in the worst way
—he loves this show.—I told him you might think about letting
him in. Come on up, Sidney. (*She bangs up.*) He didn't quite
(*Crosses* L. C.) understand at first. He was asleep.

SHRINER. Oh, I could have talked to him tomorrow.

FRANCES. Oh, no!

SHRINER.

"Oh, what a rogue and peasant slave am I,
Oh, that this too, too solid flesh would melt."

Hamlet. Did it in high school.

FRANCES. I'll bet you were just wonderful.

SHRINER. Oh, just adequate. Tell me something, Mrs. Black.
(FRANCES *steps* R.) Just what kind of play would you say this is?
I loved it, mind you, but it's a very strange play, isn't it?

FRANCES. (*Crossing a step* L.) Why, no. It's—it's an allegory.

SHRINER. Oh. I see.

STELLA. Ever see "Life with Father," Mr. Gallegher?

SHRINER. Oh, yes.

STELLA. That was an allegory.

SHRINER. Was it?

FRANCES. Sure. (*Crosses below drum table.*) "Oklahoma"? Big
allegory. (*Door opens and* SIDNEY *appears.*)

SIDNEY. (*Crossing* D. *above* L. C. *chair.*) If this is some kind of
joke I'm going to hit you both over the head with J. J.!

FRANCES. (*As* SHRINER *crosses to* SIDNEY C.) Honey, this is Mr.
William H. Gallegher. (*Sits* L. *chair.*)

SHRINER. (*Shaking him by the hand.*) Mr. Black, this is a real
privilege—to meet the man who put (STELLA *crosses to above
sofa.*) on that wonderful show! What a message! And your wife
says you agree with her about getting new people in the theater.
New faces—new blood—new money! It's a kick meeting you all,
I can tell you. I'm just a great big, stage-struck business man,
Mr. Black.

SIDNEY. (*Getting it, sits him in* R. C. *chair.*) Oh, yes! Yes! Sit
down, Mr. Gallegher! Make yourself comfortable. (*Crosses to*
FRANCES.) Did you offer Mr. Gallegher a drink, Frances?

SHRINER. No, no, thanks. Yessir, I sure liked that show tonight,
Mr. Black.

SIDNEY. (*Crossing* L. C.) Good, good. We liked it ourselves.

SHRINER. And some time when you're doing another show, Mr. Black, and you want to open the door a little and let some outside people in, I wish you'd remember William H. Gallegher from Elkhart, Indiana. Just let me know the amount and you'll get a check by return mail. And I hope you do one real soon.

SIDNEY. When I'm doing another show? I thought you liked this one so much?

SHRINER. Oh, I do. But I wouldn't come in on this one.

SIDNEY. Oh, you wouldn't! Why not?

SHRINER. Why, I just couldn't, Mr. Black. This one is a sure thing! I wouldn't want to take advantage of you!

SIDNEY. (Crossing above drum table to arm of L. chair, sits.) Take advantage of me! Trap me! Come on! Take advantage! Who cares?

SHRINER. This one's a sure thing, Mr. Black! I want to gamble!

SIDNEY. What makes you so sure this is a sure thing, my friend?

SHRINER. Why—haven't you seen the papers, Mr. Black? The morning papers?

SIDNEY. No.

SHRINER. Why, they say it's wonderful. (SIDNEY crosses below to C.) I looked at them on the way (STELLA crosses above phone table.) up in the (FRANCES rises.) elevator! They say it's great! (He takes newspapers out of his pocket. SIDNEY makes a grab for them. He reads silently for a moment. Then . . .)

SIDNEY. (Reading, at C.) " It would be inaccurate to call ' The Time Is Now ' a good play, or to suggest that the goings-on on the stage of the Colonial Theater last evening were not often puzzling, dangerously close to grotesque, and sometimes downright irritating." (He looks up.) This is supposed to be good? Are you all crazy?

SHRINER. Go on, go on! Read the rest of it!

SIDNEY. (Reading.) " Yet in spite of its awkwardness, its bewildering unwillingness to make even the simplest concession to an audience, there shines through this play, at its best moments, a kind of singing poetry, a lyric quality of exultation and hope, that make it a stirring and exciting experience." (He looks up.) We're awake, Frances! Only this is what I dreamt about! A Roman candle in the tired face of show business, that's what he's saying! A candy box full of bombs!

FRANCES. (Crossing above drum table to SIDNEY.) Keep reading,

53

sugar! Keep cutting down my loss! (*Crosses above* L. *chair.* FRANCES *and* STELLA *grab papers from him,* STELLA *crosses above phone table, and each starts to read notices simultaneously.* SID-NEY *also continues to read along with them from his notice.*)

STELLA. " Every so often in the theater a part and an actress meet on rare terms, and the result . . ."

FRANCES. " The director of Shakespeare and Chekhov has turned his back on the classical tradition and boldly given us a dazzling experiment in modern stagecraft."

SIDNEY. " The following laurel wreaths are hereby handed out with bated breath and the promise that they will turn into brickbats if the star, the author and the director do not wield a golden horsewhip and make ' The Time is Now ' live up to its best! " (*All the while they are reading the* SHRINER *is strolling from one to the other.*)

(*All To-gether.*)

STELLA. (*Picking up phone.*) Hello, Operator, get me Mr. Carleton Fitzgerald. Never mind the no-disturb. Just get him.—Hello, Carleton? Stella—now wait a minute—don't you hang up—you are *so* talking to me. The notices are good—do you hear me, Carleton? The notices are good! Hello? Yeah—well—don't cry for a couple of minutes yet and get in here. (*During this* SIDNEY *is at door,* FRANCES *and* SHRINER *above* L. *chair.*)

SIDNEY. (U. R., *as he goes to* IRENE'S *door, opens it, and calls her.*) Irene! Are you awake? (*Reading from his paper.*) " Irene Livingston covered herself with glory last night. She gave the play and the part her glorious best, and the theater this morning is richer for it." Elinor Hughes in the *Herald.*

IRENE. (*Crossing* D. *to* STELLA.) What does Elliot Norton say?

STELLA. (*She reads from other paper.*) " Every so often in the theater a part and an actress meet on rare terms." (*Crosses* D., *takes paper from* STELLA *and crosses* D. R.)

IRENE. (TYLER *enters and crosses* D. *above sofa.*) " It is this ob-server's rash guess that like Jeanne Eagels in ' Rain,' Irene Living-ston's place in that small galaxy of theatrical greats is now as-ured."—That dear man! (STELLA *sits* R. C. *chair.*)

SHRINER. (*Crossing above sofa.*) Wait till I tell Milly about this! Isn't this wonderful? Miss Livingston! This is a great honor.

SIDNEY. (*Crossing* D. *to* SHRINER, *taking him to door.*) Listen, Jack, we're very busy, thanks. Thanks very much for bringing up the papers. Call me in the morning, and I'll send you an autograph.

SHRINER. This is what I dreamed the theater would be like! Just what I dreamed the theater would be like! (*He goes.* SIDNEY *crosses* D., *sits* L. C. *chair.*)

TYLER. What's happened, Mother? Does this mean everything is all right, Irene? That we're not going duck shooting?

STELLA. I may go with you, Tyler, and just shoot ducks for the rest of my life. Because it's pretty obvious that I don't know the difference between a good play and a hole in the ground. (*Rises, crosses* U. *to bar. Pound on door.*)

TYLER. (*Above sofa.*) But, Irene! I've already wired Abercrombie and Fitch! (*Knock again.*)

STELLA. Come in! (CARLETON *enters, crosses* D. C.)

IRENE. Darling—don't move—don't speak—just listen! (*She reads.*) "Never, in a long and distinguished career, has the sensitive directorial hand of Carleton Fitzgerald wrought such pure stage magic." (*As* CARLETON *starts to choke.*) Wait, darling, wait! (*Crosses below sofa to* CARLETON C.) Don't even breathe! Just listen! (*She goes on.* FRANCES *crosses to bar.*) A major share of the credit belongs to Carleton Fitzgerald, and along with it goes this critic's huzzah of unabashed admiration." There, darling, there! What do you say to that!

CARLETON. (*Crossing to* R. C. *chair, sits. All emotion.* STELLA *crosses* D. *above* L. *chair.*) I could cry. (IRENE *crosses* U. *above sofa.*) Am I mentioned in both notices? I never read them—that's why I ask.

SIDNEY. (*Reading.*) "To write this play off as a failure, even an ambitious and daring failure, would be a lasting pity (*Rises, crosses below drum table to* D. L. FRANCES *crosses above* R. C. *chair.*) but there are in this venture the electric possibilities of breaking new ground, of making the unworkable work, of bringing a new writer of talent and distinction into the theater, and covering all concerned with glory." Mama mia! (*Kisses* STELLA.)

CARLETON. (*Rising and crossing below sofa.*) I must phone Margaret. She's leaving for New Hampshire to open the farm!

SIDNEY. (*Crossing below to* C.) Wait a minute! There's something else here!

FRANCES. Aha! Now it comes! The finger!

SIDNEY. No! It's about me! (*His face breaks into a delighted boyish grin. Then he reads again.*) "Sidney Black deserves some kind

55

of Academy Award for his wonderful courage and staggering lavishness in getting it on the stage at all."

FRANCES. Light up, Jack, tonight's the night!

SIDNEY. (*He shifts to other paper.*) The same! Only more so! The dictionary exploding in our laps, begging us not to fall on our face! Listen to this: (*He reads.*) " To paraphrase Mr. Churchill, we see nothing ahead for ' The Time is Now ' but blood, sweat, toil and tears, but with another little bow to Mr. Churchill, we should like to remind the star, the author, the director, and the producer, that this may be their finest hour. That's how good we think it could be." (*He lets papers fall to his side, and stands quite still for a moment. Then he crosses to* IRENE, *and without a word, plants a kiss on her cheek. Turning, he crosses to* CARLETON, *below sofa, and still without speaking, plants a kiss on* CARLETON'S *cheek, sits sofa* L.)

CARLETON. (TYLER *crossing* U. *in alcove.*) My whole career is passing in front of me, like the time I fell through the trap-door in " Faust "! I must sit down! (*Sits sofa* R.)

IRENE. (*Dabbing at her eyes as* STELLA *sits arm* L. *chair and crossing to above sofa.* FRANCES *sits arm of* L. C. *chair.*) Bless you, darling! Bless you both! I'm so very proud to know you! This is the last chapter of my book! I know it now! What else could it be but this? Sidney's kiss—and then just the words: " I was proud to know them." *The End.* And now, darlings, we must call Peter! He doesn't know yet! (*Crosses to below* R. C. *chair.*) Oh, that touching, dear, shining young face—I can hardly wait to see it. (*She picks up phone.*)

SIDNEY. Wait, Irene, wait! Should we disturb him? That boy will need every bit of sleep he can get. Every bit of reserve strength he's got. (*Rises, crosses* U. C.) Who's going to write those wonderful words, words that are pennies from heaven? You, me, Carleton? No, Peter. That's our blood, sweat, toil and tears! Sleep good, my boy. Tomorrow morning I'm your mother, your wife, your mistress, your messenger boy. . . . You want strawberries for breakfast with extra heavy cream? You've got 'em. I'll dip 'em in sugar and pop them in your mouth one by one. . . . (*Crosses* L.) My friends, we're going to mother him, father him, laugh with him, cry with him, (*Crosses* R.) rock him to sleep, massage him awake, buy him strange foods and if necessary strange women. (*Crosses* C.) We're going to baby him, spoil him, pamper him, love him, drink with him, smoke with him, run around

naked with him, if that's what he wants, (*Crosses above sofa to*
D. R.) because we're bailing out at ten thousand feet, and the
parachute won't open without him. It's D-Day, folks; be nice to
General Eisenhower.

CARLETON. (*Firmly kissing* SIDNEY *on both cheeks. Rising and
crossing to* SIDNEY.) One for Belasco and one for Winthrop Ames!
You're in the great tradition, Sidney Black!

SIDNEY. Thank you, Carleton. (*Crossing above to* C., CARLETON
crosses above sofa.)

FRANCES. (*Crossing to* SIDNEY *at* C.) Well, if everybody's doing
it! (*She comes to* SIDNEY *and kisses him.*) That's not for the
dough, Daddy, that's for you. You're a cock-eyed wonder, if
anyone should ask me!

IRENE. (*Rising and crossing to* SIDNEY U. C.) He's more than that,
darling! He's a wonderful human being! He has a tenderness and
understanding that makes you want to give him your best! Oh,
what a lucky woman I am to have Sidney and (CARLETON *crosses
to* IRENE *at* C.) Carleton at my side! Oh, my darlings, this must
not end! We must do everything together from (FRANCES *crosses
U. to windows*) now on! I shall never do another play without
you—never—what joy is there comparable to working with three
people who love each other very much? (*Crosses* D. R.) What else
matters? Applause—notices—failure—success—pouff! I give
them to you! Give me comrades (SIDNEY *and* CARLETON *cross
above sofa.*) that's all I ask—two good companions! And I've got
them, my darlings, I've got them! Oh, Sidney, please! Can't we
call Peter? (*Sits sofa.*) Can't we start to work tonight—now!

SIDNEY. All right—rest—sleep—all that comes later! Synchronize
your watches, folks—here comes ten days that are going to shake
show business. (*He picks up phone.*) Get me Mr. Peter Sloan. If
there's a no-disturb—ring him anyway—I'll take the responsibility!
Huh? What did you say? Repeat that again, will you, operator!
You're sure! Okay! (*He hangs up.*) He checked out. About an
hour ago! He's gone!

CARLETON. What!

IRENE. (*Rising.*) What do you mean, checked out?

FRANCES. (*Crossing* D. *above* L. C. *chair.*) She must be wrong,
Sidney—she didn't get the right name!

STELLA. Where did he go?

IRENE. It's a mistake, Sidney—it must be a mistake!

SIDNEY. It's no mistake. He's gone!

57

IRENE. But why? What does this mean?

SIDNEY. Hold it, everybody, please! I'm trying to think on my feet
—fast. (OWEN and MISS LOWELL enter.) Were you with Peter,
Owen? You know about this?

OWEN. (Closing door.) Yes. (MISS LOWELL crosses above sofa to
desk chair, sits.)

SIDNEY. Where is he?

OWEN. (Crossing D. to L. C. chair, sits.) We left him at the airport. He's taking the four-thirty plane to New York to pick up his
girl, and tomorrow afternoon he'll be in Wisconsin.

SIDNEY. (Into phone.) Get me the airport.

IRENE. (Crossing to OWEN.) But what happened? Did somebody
frighten him? Did he go out of his mind suddenly?

CARLETON. But how could he just leave? Why didn't somebody
stop him? Did he know about the notices?

OWEN. Yes, he read them at the airport.

MISS LOWELL. They didn't seem to matter to him at all.

IRENE. (Crossing D. R.) Darling, this is a joke! Some horrible, un-
funny joke and I want it stopped at once. Do you hear?

SIDNEY. Irene, please, this is no joke. . . . Get me the manager.
(IRENE sits R. end sofa.) The manager is a big friend of mine.
Remember when the Senate investigated the airlines last summer?
. . . Owes me a favor. Hello, Walter, Sidney Black. Yes, yes, I'm
fine. Yeah, it's good to be in Boston. Listen, Walter. Remember
what you told me in Union Station last summer? Well, now I'm
ready. There's a guy going out on the four-thirty plane. Peter
Sloan is the name. I need him back here. How? Throw him off
the plane and get one of your special deputies to bring him over
here to the Ritz. No, no, don't worry about false arrest. I'll take
the responsibility. Thanks, Walter. This squares us until the next
investigation.—Why did he go, Owen, do you know? (Crosses D.
to OWEN.)

OWEN. (Rising and crossing U. to bar.) He left a note for you,
Sidney. I believe it's for all of you. (He takes letter out of his
pocket and hands it to SIDNEY, who tears it open, crosses to sofa,
sits, as IRENE and CARLETON go to him and read it over his shoul-
der.)

FRANCES. What the hell goes on, Stella! A minute ago we were in
the bag!

STELLA. (Sitting L. chair.) Yeah, and now they're pulling up the
zipper.

TYLER. How can a man just walk out? Isn't there a union or something?

OWEN. Indeed there is. I'm the President of it.

FRANCES. (*To* SIDNEY.) Well, what does it say? Had to go to his grandmother's funeral or something?

SIDNEY. Not that good an excuse. This letter was either written by a tired baby or an excited drunk. That kid's gone crazy! This is a Sunday (*Rises.*) school sermon—an editorial in the Holy Rollers' Gazette! Did you read it, Owen? (*Crosses* U. C.)

OWEN. No, but I have a fairly good idea of what it says.

IRENE. (*Rising.*) It's unbelievable! Accusing us of pettiness and selfishness! Why, I slaved to get this play on! (*Gives note to* CARLETON.) I practically crawled on my belly to Sidney Black to get the money! What is he talking about? (*Crosses* D. R.)

CARLETON. What does he mean "strange insincerities you call loyalties"? Didn't I postpone my wife's play? Didn't I weep with joy and humility through every rehearsal? What does he mean?

SIDNEY. What does he mean? What does a man in an asylum mean when he says "Look—I'm a teapot—pour me!" Do you answer him? Can you reason with a child who says "The bogey man is on my bed!" (*Crosses* D. L.) God Almighty, what a time for a guy to go off his rocker! He picks the opening night to go berserk! He couldn't wait ten days!

OWEN. You think that's what it is, Sidney? (*Crosses* D. *to* L. C. *chair, sits.*)

SIDNEY. Think? What else is it? (*Crosses* U. *to windows.*)

IRENE. (*Crossing* U. *to door.*) It's utter lunacy, that's what it is!

CARLETON. We should have known it. We should have known he was crazy.

OWEN. (*Crossing* D. *to* L. C. *chair, sits.*) Well, that makes it easier for all of you, at any rate.

SIDNEY. (*Crossing* D. *to sofa, sits.*) Easier! We're trapped like rats. What do you mean—easier!

OWEN. It's always easier to blame it on the author. I'll never quite understand how George Bernard Shaw has lived to be ninety.

IRENE. (*Crossing* D. *to* OWEN.) Darling, you're not suggesting he's right, are you?

OWEN. No. I think he should have stayed. (IRENE *crosses* U. *to door.*) I did my best to make him stay. I tried to explain, in a quiet way, the difference between you people and John Dillinger. I didn't succeed.

59

SIDNEY. Are you crazy? Are all authors crazy?

OWEN. A little. No sane person could stand this for long. But Sloan isn't crazy, Sidney. There's something touching and young and rather admirable about him. And I'm not even sure he isn't right.

SIDNEY. Right about what? What did we destroy? (*Rising and crossing* C.) His play? Him? Because a few snappy words were exchanged? Is that it? Because we were all trying to save our necks, and his, too, for that matter! (*Crosses below sofa.*) What were we supposed to do—hit the trail and be saved—get religion or something? What are you handing out? A new commandment?

OWEN. No. It's just that he's found out we're dubious people— and he can't accept that. (*Rises and crosses* D. L.) Me—I made my bed with you a long time ago—I'm one of you—I even enjoy it now. (SIDNEY *sits sofa.*) But we've all forgotten what it is to be young, to be sensitive, and to be hurt. This was his (*Crosses* L. C.) first play—his baby—and you were its mother and father all rolled into one. Well, the baby was born and it wasn't a very pretty child. So what did Mama and Papa do? (*Crosses to* R. C. *chair, sits.*) They kicked it in the head—stepped on it—and threw it out the window. What do you expect, Sidney? Flowers?

IRENE. You're (*Crossing* D. L. C.) unfair, Owen. You're bitterly unfair. We loved this play—we always have. We knew what a chance it was —— (*Sits* L. C. *chair.*)

SIDNEY. And we blew it! He's right! We blew it—all of us. Nobody more than me! The only thing he didn't say was that we deserve this—we deserve that kid walking out on us—to hell with whether he's right or wrong or crazy. We deserve it! You know something, Owen? (FRANCES *slowly crosses* U. *to bar.*) You know what makes it funny? This was the one time I wasn't showing off —showing the world how smart I was—this was something I was doing for myself—putting my chips down quietly on the one thing that always had me bug-eyed with wonder and respect—talent— like Sloan's. It's maybe the first time in my life I ever did something like this—for my insides—for me—to be a big man to myself. Just that and nothing else. And I blew it. So I guess I won't keep on kidding myself any more.

FRANCES. (*Crossing to above sofa.*) You keep right on, Sidney. With every cent I've got or you've got. And that includes this junk—and hocking those ice skates if necessary.

SIDNEY. Shut up, Frances. (*Rises, kisses* FRANCES. *Phone rings.*)
Yes. Yeah! Okay. (*He hangs up.*) Peter's coming up!

IRENE. He's back!

CARLETON. Wonderful! Wonderful!

SIDNEY. I don't think we've got much chance. Folks, will you just
leave the three of us alone to talk to him?

OWEN. Gladly, Sidney, I'd like to see you and Robert E. Sherwood
mixed up together! (*Rises, crosses* U. *to alcove door, exits.*) Good
luck, Sidney. I'd like to see him stay.

STELLA. (*Rises, exits* D. L.) I'll deal 'em up inside. This is our last
round, I guess.

FRANCES. Keep swinging, Daddy. You're my boy! (*Crosses to*
IRENE, L. C. *chair.*) Don't worry, Irene, if anybody can make him
stay, Sidney can pull it off. (*Exits* D. L. *All exit except* SIDNEY,
CARLETON *and* IRENE.)

SIDNEY. Irene, Carleton—no tricks. The only chance we got with
this kid is to go down on our knees and beg. (*Knock on door.*)
Now, remember! (*They nod.* IRENE *crosses* D. L., CARLETON D. R.
Knock on door again.) Come in! (SIDNEY *crosses* U. R. C. *A
plain-clothes cop comes in with* PETER U. C.—*holding him by the
arm—collar, tie awry, hat jammed down, and* PETER *white with
rage.*)

COP. Here he is, Mr. Black, is that all you want?

SIDNEY. Yes.

COP. I don't know. Do you think you can handle him? He's given
me lots of trouble.

PETER. That's all right, Officer. I'm sorry I was a little rough. I
won't be any more trouble. (COP *goes out.*) Well, Mr. Black,
you're not only running show business, you're running the country
as well.

SIDNEY. Sorry about the cops, Peter. But we had to get you back
and talk to you.

PETER. That's all right, Sidney. I'm delighted to have the chance
to see you face to face and tell you what I think of you.

IRENE. (*Crossing above* L. *chair.*) Peter—we behaved contempti-
bly! We know it—there is no excuse for us.

CARLETON. We were frightened and hysterical. Panic-stricken.
Can you understand that?

SIDNEY. We don't expect you to forgive us or forget anything.
Just give us a chance to work together and make it live.

PETER. I read the notices, too. Now you're willing to do anything, aren't you? Well, I'm not. There are things more important to me than having a hit.

SIDNEY. (*Quietly.*) What are they, Peter?

PETER. Principles, for one thing. Decency, for another.

SIDNEY. We got principles, too, Peter. You don't think so, but we got 'em. One of them is to do the best we can in the toughest business in the world.

IRENE. A cutthroat, heart-breaking business, Peter. Decency is a luxury we can't always afford. Or we forget sometimes.

CARLETON. You have the cruelty of innocence, Peter. You don't know what people like Irene, Sidney and myself have had to go through to get where we are.

PETER. Oh, yes, I do. I saw you all go through it an hour ago. Quite a spectacle.

IRENE. All right—we disappoint you! We loved your play and then we turned on it. That's the way we are—you saw our best and our worst. That's human, isn't it? What about you? What about *your* faith? Was it all just talk you wrote in the play, or doesn't it stand up any better than ours did?

SIDNEY. Sh-sh! Irene! It's over! We'll take our lumps like little gentlemen! (CARLETON *sits sofa.*) Next time, Peter, don't try and judge everybody from way up there—but from down here where the rest of us are scrambling around trying to live. I understand —and what's more, I don't blame you. You thought we were heroes—we ain't. Then you thought we were heavies—we ain't exactly that, either. We're mixed up altogether like everybody else. (*Crosses above sofa.*) You'll learn. I wish you'd found out with somebody else—but good luck, kid!

PETER. (*He laughs shortly.*) You don't fool me for a minute, Sidney. None of you do. You'll do anything, say anything, try anything to get what you want!

SIDNEY. (*Goes to desk* D. R., *writes paper.*) " I, Sidney Black, do hereby release all my rights in Peter Sloan's play, ' The Time is Now,' and all rights whatsoever are hereby returned to him." (*Crosses above sofa to* PETER, C., *hands him paper.*) Okay. You got your play back. And this gives me the privilege of telling you just what I think of you. You write like an angel, but you're a bit of a jerk. And maybe a little yellow, too. You turned just as much as we did—even more—you walked out on yourself. Okay. You got your play. What are you waiting for? Get on your plane. (*Crosses to* L. C. *chair. Sits.*)

PETER. (*Looking at paper, laughs.*) Well, now I've seen everything. This is the biggest switch of all.

SIDNEY. (*Indignant.*) Switch! What do you mean switch? Go on. Get out of here.

PETER. (*Crossing D. C.*) And I've got one for you. I've learned one thing out of dealing with Murder, Inc. If I'm going to work and live in the theater and say what I want to say, it's got to be with people—all kinds of people—even people like you. So there'll be no laughing it up—no Olson and Johnson—and no idiotic shenanigans from you, or you, or you. Especially you. You crazy little bastard.

SIDNEY. (*Rising and hugging him, crossing U. C.*) Peter, darling, this is my type talk! This I understand. (CARLETON *rises, crossing above sofa.*)

PETER. (*Pushing his arms away.*) But watch out—all of you. I've just graduated! I've got diploma scars all over me. Now, let's get to work! (*Crosses to R. C. chair, sits,* SIDNEY *crosses D. L.*)

SIDNEY. (*Crossing D. below to L.*) All right! Act One. Scene One! Let's fix the show! (PETER *crosses to R. C. chair, sits.*)

IRENE. (*Crossing to* PETER.) Oh, bless you, darling, you know how I love this play—how I'd give my life for it—but I cannot have three hundred sweaty extras lying on top of me during ——

CARLETON. (*Crossing C.*) If you'd stay in the place you're supposed to stay in, Irene, instead of wandering all over the damn stage, you wouldn't ——

SIDNEY. Let the woman finish a sentence, can't you?

CARLETON. (*Crossing to* SIDNEY D. L.) Just a moment, Mr. Black —my contract says you are not to even talk to me unless I allow it, and I have no intention of tearing the contract up, believe me! I can also bar you from the theater. (*Crosses across stage to* D. L. *Everyone enters.*)

PETER. (*Rising.*) Shut up! Shut up, all of you, shut up. I'll tell you what's wrong with that first scene. Shut up and let the man who wrote it tell you. (*Crosses to sofa, sits.*) Now, come on, all of you.

IRENE. (*Crossing to sofa.*) Oh, bless you, darling—if you can just fix the first scene, I'm sure everything else will.

SIDNEY. (*Crossing to* IRENE.) Sh! Irene! Do you interrupt a salmon swimming upstream? Do you interrupt Dr. Ehrlich at experiment 605? Talk, Peter, talk! Take a wire (*Crosses above sofa to desk.*) to Lee Shubert, Miss Lowell: " Dear Lee, I want

two weeks in Philadelphia, two in Detroit and two in Pittsburgh! "
(*Crosses* D. L.)

STELLA. Six more weeks of gin, Frances!

CARLETON. (*Crossing below coffee table, sits on floor.*) I could cry!

FRANCES. (*Calling across room.*) Daddy—it's the same old story!
You're coming out of that sewer covered with honey!

CURTAIN

WORKING PROPERTY PLOT

Act I

On Stage
Cigarettes, matches, ashtrays

On Coffee Table
White and yellow stationery
Typewriter, typing paper
Phone book under typewriter
Title page, pencil

On Piano, Against Bar
Flower boxes, bouquets of flowers

On Piano
Telegrams, hand mirror

On Desk
Pencils, pens, white stationery
Typing paper
One ashtray

On Drum Table
Vase of flowers
Playing cards, score pad
Two pencils (one hidden in flower vase)

Parrot, parrot cage (cover open)

On Bar
One bottle Vat 69
One bottle brandy
Two bottles bourbon
Two bottles soda (uncapped)
12 glasses (half full)
Three shot glasses

Phone Table
Orchid corsage in transparent box
Piano stool under piano

Off Stage—Center
L—One hat box (Frances)
L—One package, gift wrapped (Sidney)
C—One suitcase (Tyler)
L—Copy of Variety, and telegrams (Stella)
Right
Massage table (Sven)
Glass beads

Act II

During Intermission
Strike used glasses, typewriter, phone book, suitcase, Variety, telegrams (flower box from phone table on piano), strike gift box (Sidney) from settee in alcove

On Stage
Move desk chair to below desk
Cover open on parrot cage
Cigarette with pin in it (on piano)
Matches on piano

Check ashtray on desk
On Bar
5 large glasses
3 shot glasses
Piano stool in front of piano

Off Stage—Center
6 balloons (inflated on string), Irene

Right
Ice bag (Tyler)
Fez—tin horns, noise makers

During Intermission
Set desk chair above desk
Strike used glasses, balloons—ice
    bag

On Bar
Set empty Vat 69 bottle (corked)
2 half full glasses

2 half empty glasses
3 shot glasses

Off Stage—Right
Fez
Three newspapers
Note in envelope
Pencil in manuscript

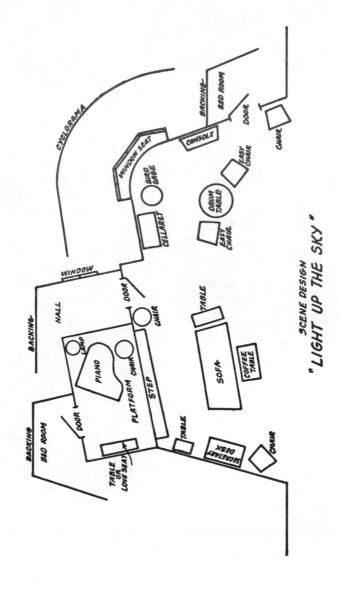

SCENE DESIGN
"LIGHT UP THE SKY"

NEW PLAYS

★ **THE EXONERATED by Jessica Blank and Erik Jensen.** Six interwoven stories paint a picture of an American criminal justice system gone horribly wrong and six brave souls who persevered to survive it. "The #1 play of the year...intense and deeply affecting..." *–NY Times.* "Riveting. Simple, honest storytelling that demands reflection." *–A.P.* "Artful and moving...pays tribute to the resilience of human hearts and minds." *–Variety.* "Stark...riveting...cunningly orchestrated." *–The New Yorker.* "Hard-hitting, powerful, and socially relevant." *–Hollywood Reporter.* [7M, 3W] ISBN: 0-8222-1946-8

★ **STRING FEVER by Jacquelyn Reingold.** Lily juggles the big issues: turning forty, artificial insemination and the elusive scientific Theory of Everything in this Off-Broadway comedy hit. "Applies the elusive rules of string theory to the conundrums of one woman's love life. Think *Sex and the City* meets *Copenhagen.*" *–NY Times.* "A funny offbeat and touching look at relationships...an appealing romantic comedy populated by oddball characters." *–NY Daily News.* "Where kooky, zany, and madcap meet...whimsically winsome." *–NY Magazine.* "STRING FEVER will have audience members happily stringing along." *–TheaterMania.com.* "Reingold's language is surprising, inventive, and unique." *–nytheatre.com.* "...[a] whimsical comic voice." *–Time Out.* [3M, 3W (doubling)] ISBN: 0-8222-1952-2

★ **DEBBIE DOES DALLAS adapted by Erica Schmidt, composed by Andrew Sherman, conceived by Susan L. Schwartz.** A modern morality tale told as a comic musical of tragic proportions as the classic film is brought to the stage. "A scream! A saucy, tongue-in-cheek romp." *–The New Yorker.* "Hilarious! DEBBIE manages to have it all: beauty, brains and a great sense of humor!" *–Time Out.* "Shamelessly silly, shrewdly self-aware and proud of being naughty. Great fun!" *–NY Times.* "Racy and raucous, a lighthearted, fast-paced thoroughly engaging and hilarious send-up." *–NY Daily News.* [3M, 5W] ISBN: 0-8222-1955-7

★ **THE MYSTERY PLAYS by Roberto Aguirre-Sacasa.** Two interrelated one acts, loosely based on the tradition of the medieval mystery plays. "... stylish, spine-tingling...Mr. Aguirre-Sacasa uses standard tricks of horror stories, borrowing liberally from masters like Kafka, Lovecraft, Hitchcock...But his mastery of the genre is his own...irresistible." *–NY Times.* "Undaunted by the special-effects limitations of theatre, playwright and *Marvel* comic-book writer Roberto Aguirre-Sacasa maps out some creepy twilight zones in THE MYSTERY PLAYS, an engaging, related pair of one acts...The theatre may rarely deliver shocks equivalent to, say, *Dawn of the Dead*, but Aguirre-Sacasa's work is fine compensation." *–Time Out.* [4M, 2W] ISBN: 0-8222-2038-5

★ **THE JOURNALS OF MIHAIL SEBASTIAN by David Auburn.** This epic one-man play spans eight tumultuous years and opens a uniquely personal window on the Romanian Holocaust and the Second World War. "Powerful." *–NY Times.* "[THE JOURNALS OF MIHAIL SEBASTIAN] allows us to glimpse the idiosyncratic effects of that awful history on one intelligent, pragmatic, recognizably real man..." *–NY Newsday.* [3M, 5W] ISBN: 0-8222-2006-7

★ **LIVING OUT by Lisa Loomer.** The story of the complicated relationship between a Salvadoran nanny and the Anglo lawyer she works for. "A stellar new play. Searingly funny." *–The New Yorker.* "Both generous and merciless, equally enjoyable and disturbing." *–NY Newsday.* "A bitingly funny new comedy. The plight of working mothers is explored from two pointedly contrasting perspectives in this sympathetic, sensitive new play." *–Variety.* [2M, 6W] ISBN: 0-8222-1994-8

DRAMATISTS PLAY SERVICE, INC.
440 Park Avenue South, New York, NY 10016   212-683-8960   Fax 212-213-1539
postmaster@dramatists.com   www.dramatists.com

NEW PLAYS

★ **MATCH by Stephen Belber.** Mike and Lisa Davis interview a dancer and choreographer about his life, but it is soon evident that their agenda will either ruin or inspire them— and definitely change their lives forever. "Prolific laughs and ear-to-ear smiles." *–NY Magazine.* "Uproariously funny, deeply moving, enthralling theater. Stephen Belber's MATCH has great beauty and tenderness, and abounds in wit." *–NY Daily News.* "Three and a half out of four stars." *–USA Today.* "A theatrical steeplechase that leads straight from outrageous bitchery to unadorned, heartfelt emotion." *–Wall Street Journal.* [2M, 1W] ISBN: 0-8222-2020-2

★ **HANK WILLIAMS: LOST HIGHWAY by Randal Myler and Mark Harelik.** The story of the beloved and volatile country-music legend Hank Williams, featuring twenty-five of his most unforgettable songs. "[LOST HIGHWAY has] the exhilarating feeling of Williams on stage in a particular place on a particular night…serves up classic country with the edges raw and the energy hot…By the end of the play, you've traveled on a profound emotional journey: LOST HIGHWAY transports its audience and communicates the inspiring message of the beauty and richness of Williams' songs…forceful, clear-eyed, moving, impressive." *–Rolling Stone.* "…honors a very particular musical talent with care and energy… smart, sweet, poignant." *–NY Times.* [7M, 3W] ISBN: 0-8222-1985-9

★ **THE STORY by Tracey Scott Wilson.** An ambitious black newspaper reporter goes against her editor to investigate a murder and finds the *best* story…but at what cost? "A singular new voice…deeply emotional, deeply intellectual, and deeply musical…" *–The New Yorker.* "…a conscientious and absorbing new drama…" *–NY Times.* "…a riveting, tough-minded drama about race, reporting and the truth…" *–A.P.* "… a stylish, attention-holding script that ends on a chilling note that will leave viewers with much to talk about." *–Curtain Up.* [2M, 7W (doubling, flexible casting)] ISBN: 0-8222-1998-0

★ **OUR LADY OF 121st STREET by Stephen Adly Guirgis.** The body of Sister Rose, beloved Harlem nun, has been stolen, reuniting a group of life-challenged childhood friends who square off as they wait for her return. "A scorching and dark new comedy… Mr. Guirgis has one of the finest imaginations for dialogue to come along in years." *–NY Times.* "Stephen Guirgis may be the best playwright in America under forty." *–NY Magazine.* [8M, 4W] ISBN: 0-8222-1965-4

★ **HOLLYWOOD ARMS by Carrie Hamilton and Carol Burnett.** The coming-of-age story of a dreamer who manages to escape her bleak life and follow her romantic ambitions to stardom. Based on Carol Burnett's bestselling autobiography, *One More Time.* "…pure theatre and pure entertainment…" *–Talkin' Broadway.* "…a warm, fuzzy evening of theatre." *–BrodwayBeat.com.* "…chuckles and smiles of recognition or surprise flow naturally…a remarkable slice of life." *–TheatreScene.net.* [5M, 5W, 1 girl] ISBN: 0-8222-1959-X

★ **INVENTING VAN GOGH by Steven Dietz.** A haunting and hallucinatory drama about the making of art, the obsession to create and the fine line that separates truth from myth. "Like a van Gogh painting, Dietz's story is a gorgeous example of excess—one that remakes reality with broad, well-chosen brush strokes. At evening's end, we're left with the author's resounding opinions on art and artifice, and provoked by his constant query into which is greater: van Gogh's art or his violent myth." *–Phoenix New Times.* "Dietz's writing is never simple. It is always brilliant. Shaded, compressed, direct, lucid—he frames his subject with a remarkable understanding of painting as a physical experience." *–Tucson Citizen.* [4M, 1W] ISBN: 0-8222-1954-9

DRAMATISTS PLAY SERVICE, INC.
440 Park Avenue South, New York, NY 10016 212-683-8960 Fax 212-213-1539
postmaster@dramatists.com www.dramatists.com

NEW PLAYS

★ **INTIMATE APPAREL by Lynn Nottage.** The moving and lyrical story of a turn-of-the-century black seamstress whose gifted hands and sewing machine are the tools she uses to fashion her dreams from the whole cloth of her life's experiences. "...Nottage's play has a delicacy and eloquence that seem absolutely right for the time she is depicting..." –*NY Daily News.* "...thoughtful, affecting...The play offers poignant commentary on an era when the cut and color of one's dress—and of course, skin—determined whom one could and could not marry, sleep with, even talk to in public." –*Variety.* [2M, 4W] ISBN: 0-8222-2009-1

★ **BROOKLYN BOY by Donald Margulies.** A witty and insightful look at what happens to a writer when his novel hits the bestseller list. "The characters are beautifully drawn, the dialogue sparkles..." –*nytheatre.com.* "Few playwrights have the mastery to smartly investigate so much through a laugh-out-loud comedy that combines the vintage subject matter of successful writer-returning-to-ethnic-roots with the familiar mid-life crisis." –*Show Business Weekly.* [4M, 3W] ISBN: 0-8222-2074-1

★ **CROWNS by Regina Taylor.** Hats become a springboard for an exploration of black history and identity in this celebratory musical play. "Taylor pulls off a Hat Trick: She scores thrice, turning CROWNS into an artful amalgamation of oral history, fashion show, and musical theater..." –*TheatreMania.com.* "...wholly theatrical...Ms. Taylor has created a show that seems to arise out of spontaneous combustion, as if a bevy of department-store customers simultaneously decided to stage a revival meeting in the changing room." –*NY Times.* [1M, 6W (2 musicians)] ISBN: 0-8222-1963-8

★ **EXITS AND ENTRANCES by Athol Fugard.** The story of a relationship between a young playwright on the threshold of his career and an aging actor who has reached the end of his. "[Fugard] can say more with a single line than most playwrights convey in an entire script...Paraphrasing the title, it's safe to say this drama, making its memorable entrance into our consciousness, is unlikely to exit as long as a theater exists for exceptional work." –*Variety.* "A thought-provoking, elegant and engrossing new play..." –*Hollywood Reporter.* [2M] ISBN: 0-8222-2041-5

★ **BUG by Tracy Letts.** A thriller featuring a pair of star-crossed lovers in an Oklahoma City motel facing a bug invasion, paranoia, conspiracy theories and twisted psychological motives. "...obscenely exciting...top-flight craftsmanship. Buckle up and brace yourself..." –*NY Times.* "...[a] thoroughly outrageous and thoroughly entertaining play...the possibility of enemies, real and imagined, to squash has never been more theatrical." –*A.P.* [3M, 2W] ISBN: 0-8222-2016-4

★ **THOM PAIN (BASED ON NOTHING) by Will Eno.** An ordinary man muses on childhood, yearning, disappointment and loss, as he draws the audience into his last-ditch plea for empathy and enlightenment. "It's one of those treasured nights in the theater—treasured nights anywhere, for that matter—that can leave you both breathless with exhilaration and...in a puddle of tears." –*NY Times.* "Eno's words...are familiar, but proffered in a way that is constantly contradictory to our expectations. Beckett is certainly among his literary ancestors." –*nytheatre.com.* [1M] ISBN: 0-8222-2076-8

★ **THE LONG CHRISTMAS RIDE HOME by Paula Vogel.** Past, present and future collide on a snowy Christmas Eve for a troubled family of five. "...[a] lovely and hauntingly original family drama...a work that breathes so much life into the theater." –*Time Out.* "...[a] delicate visual feast..." –*NY Times.* "...brutal and lovely...the overall effect is magical." –*NY Newsday.* [3M, 3W] ISBN: 0-8222-2003-2

DRAMATISTS PLAY SERVICE, INC.
440 Park Avenue South, New York, NY 10016 212-683-8960 Fax 212-213-1539
postmaster@dramatists.com www.dramatists.com